Iain MacKenzie
Resistance and the Politics of Truth

Iain MacKenzie is a co-director of the Centre for Critical Thought and a senior lecturer in Politics at the University of Kent. His research focusses on poststructuralism and political philosophy.

Iain MacKenzie

# Resistance and the Politics of Truth

## Foucault, Deleuze, Badiou

[transcript]

© 2018 transcript Verlag, Bielefeld

**Bibliographic information published by the Deutsche Nationalbibliothek**

The Deutsche Nationalbibliothek lists this publication in the Deutsche Nationalbibliografie; detailed bibliographic data are available in the Internet at http://dnb.d-nb.de

Cover layout: Kordula Röckenhaus, Bielefeld
Printed by Majuskel Medienproduktion GmbH, Wetzlar
Print-ISBN 978-3-8376-3907-0
PDF-ISBN 978-3-8394-3907-4
EPUB-ISBN 978-3-7328-3907-0

# Contents

# Acknowledgements

This book is the result of many conversations over the years, largely within the framework of a module that I have taught that bears the same title. My thanks to all the students who have contributed to our discussions in seminars and who, in ways that are too imperceptible for me to know, have helped shape my understanding of the key themes of resistance, politics and truth. For their close and generous readings of an early draft of this book, I thank Ben Turner, Chris Henry and Gaby Hernandez. For all his editorial work on this project, which has been a model of thorough and meticulous engagement throughout, Jakob Horstmann has my deep thanks. My co-conspirator in theory, Robert Porter, has been a constant companion and friend as this book has taken shape and I am particularly thankful for his agreement that I could use small sections of our co-authored unpublished work in the Introduction and final chapter. To my children, Kathryn and Sam, whose love and support through the tricky stages of the book's gestation was invaluable in so many ways, thanks are not enough. For her unwavering capacity for understanding and her sharp intellect, all of which made this project possible, I dedicate the book to Anna Cutler, in love and in life.

# Introduction: A Time to Think and Act Differently?

'The truth will set you free' is a maxim that has been and remains central to both theories and practices of resistance. Often, and with just cause, we think that the regimes of domination and oppression from which we wish to be liberated are those based on lies: lies about who we are that form the bedrock of a whole series of economic, social and political formations that discriminate against us on the basis of class, gender, sexual orientation, nationality, cultural practices and so on. With this thought firmly in our minds, and the lies exposed, we are able to muster the forces of resistance to overthrow or to call to account those regimes that have dominated our lives. Of course, resistance more often than not requires commitment and courage, because those who benefit from the lies never want to give up the power that their lies afford them, but with the truth firmly at our side we endure and persevere knowing that one day we will be victorious and our time of freedom will come; if not for us then at least for those that will follow in our footsteps. It is a powerful and profoundly motivating image of the relationship between resistance, politics and truth: but is it too simple because too dogmatic?

What if there is a politics to truth? If every attempt to articulate the truth is already implicated in a political perspective then it is by no means obvious that we will become free by simply discovering the truth about that which oppresses us. If we are guided by the idea that the truth can be set against oppressive political regimes are we often forgetting the political perspective that motivates our own understanding of what counts as the truth? Of course, we may not be so naïve as to think that what counts as the truth is neutral with respect to politics, and we may defend the idea that our political perspective is the one that will make us, and everyone, truly free. But this already complicates the image and forces us to think about why our perspective and not another is the true source of our liberation. Moreover, one of the historical problems we have to face is that we are prone to forgetting that what we think is freedom may in fact be a new form of oppression, for us and/or for others. Such is a typically liberal concern with the revolutionary movements that characterised the twentieth century. But it is also a concern for those in the civil rights movements that have witnessed their liberatory agendas being subsumed within new, and sometimes more subtle and more pervasive, forms of domination within liberal democracies. In general terms, perhaps the truth will not set us free and it is the idea of truth itself that must be resisted because one way or another we will always end up in states of oppression if we mobilise behind it. Understandably, such scepticism with regard to the traditional image of the relationship between resistance, politics and truth may have us shrugging in acceptance of the status quo: but is that too defeatist because too sceptical?

Is it possible to move beyond the dogmatic simplicity of the traditional image without accepting the sceptical defeatism that may result from quickly embracing a more complicated image? This question is the start of a more *critical* appreciation of the relationship between truth, freedom and resistance. Putting it this way, however, is to acknowledge that much of Enlightenment and post-Enlightenment social and political thought has been motivated by the desire to understand the relationship between these terms. That said, it remains the case that most modern thinkers in the Enlightenment tradition have resolved this relationship on the side of variously nuanced versions of the traditional image, while some, more occasionally, have resolved it on the side of similarly nuanced forms of defeatism. Very few theoretical positions have embraced the challenge of a non-dogmatic and non-defeatist understanding of the relationship between resistance, politics and truth; which is to say that very few theorists have sought both to provide good grounds for practices of resistance and to accept that truth is always already implicated in the regimes of domination that those practices hope to overthrow. Two relatively recent theoretical positions that take this challenge seriously are the poststructuralist and post-foundational political philosophies that have emerged during the second half of the twentieth century. Of course, they continue to inspire admiration and condemnation in almost equal measure both from those who defend traditional notions of truth in some form and from those who espouse defeatism in some form. But what they offer, alongside many contributions they contain, is a way of thinking about the relationship between truth, politics and resistance that prioritises the connection of these terms through the idea of the event. In other words, they ask: *what happens* in practices of resistance? And, how does understanding what happens in and through practices of resistance give us *grounds* to develop a complex image of the politics of truth such that we can be optimistic rather than defeatist? However, while both perspectives have developed event-oriented philosophies – that view the category of the event as ontologically primary and politically powerful – that purport to do both of these things, they have conceived of this in competing ways. The main theme of this book is to understand the relationship between truth, politics and resistance as *an evental relationship*, through consideration of both poststructuralist and post-foundationalist perspectives.

These two political philosophies will frame discussion of major thinkers of the 20th and 21st Centuries; with a particular focus on Foucault, Deleuze and Badiou. While these three thinkers offer competing answers to the guiding questions they are also linked by virtue of their emphasis upon the importance of the category of 'the event' when thinking about truth and also what we can hope to do to resist. Having explored these different yet overlapping perspectives it will be argued that a critically-oriented reading of poststructuralists (such as Foucault and Deleuze), one that places their work firmly within the Kantian legacy of modern philosophy, provides the grounds for practices of resistance that the post-foundational thinkers (such as Badiou) have eviscerated in the name of a renewed faith in truth, albeit a radically new conception of what it is to be a subject of truth. To prefigure the conclusion, one that will require some deft weaving through these three thinkers, the upshot of this is that a critically oriented poststructuralist position provides the grounds for sustainable practices of resistance against domination if we understand what happens in such practices as *an art of the event*. The, perhaps surprising, turn to art will be explained as the discussion unfolds, as will many of the just suspicions this turn may engender. What it offers, however, is a way out of the stalemate between simple dogmatism and complex scepticism in the name of a genuinely critical account of how practices of resistance can be informed by a politics of truth.

Before embarking on the journey, however, it is important to specify what is meant in this context by poststructuralism and post-foundationalism, not least because this will help to clarify what is at stake in framing the discussion through these two theoretical positions. As with any 'ism' these two have competing and not always harmonious definitions attached to them. In the remainder of this introduction, I will specify what I mean by these terms, their similarities and how they differ. Once we have a better grasp of what exactly is at stake then we will be able to articulate the defining problems of the argument to follow in more precise terms and why it is the case that for the key thinkers to be discussed below that ours is a time when it is necessary to think and act differently in the world if we are to find the resources to sustain our practices of resistance.

Poststructuralism is a development of the structuralist critique of humanism that tries to avoid the pitfalls that beset structuralism. But what does this mean? Starting with humanism, we can say that it has been the animating, even dominant, assumption behind many modern and Enlightenment-inspired philosophies in general, not just political philosophies. The guiding humanist presumptions are that humans are at the centre of the world in terms of what we know about the world and how we know what we know about the world. Furthermore, once the centrality of a human-centred epistemology has been established, then human beings are deemed able to control both 'outer nature' and our 'inner worlds', bringing both into our rational orbit and thereby expunging all the legacies of Aristotelian and scholastic obfuscation. For humanists, the human is the centre of all meaningful activity because it is the human that brings meaning to all things. It is the human that is the beginning and also the end or purpose of all philosophical reflection.

For the structuralists, this focus on humans blinded us to the fact that there are deep structures that shape our sense of ourselves, what we know and how we know what we know, but also that shape our sense of purpose, meaningfulness and value. Indeed, for some of the structuralists, this project was at least initially conceived as a scientific project aimed at removing the lingering theological and ideological problems brought into being by assuming that humans are, in a God-like fashion, at the centre of everything. Claude Levi-Straus, for example, said that 'structuralism reveals, behind phenomena, a unity and coherence that could not be brought about by a simple description of the facts' (1981: 68); a simple description by us humans of the facts 'for us'. Typically, structuralists placed language itself rather than the human at the centre of things, but in a manner that meant that language was not to be viewed as a set of words each with their own individual meaning for humans, but as a system of interlocking elements that functioned by virtue of the differences between them regardless of our intentions. 'Cat' does not simply refer to a furry animal in front of the fire as decided by human intention, rather it functions as a meaningful word because it is not 'dog' or 'mouse' etc, and it is the way these differences function in language systems that is to be understood if we are to figure out why they are meaningful terms at all. As Terence Hawkes explains, for structuralists, 'the true nature of things may be said to lie not in the things themselves, but in the relationships which we construct, and then perceive, between them' (1977: 17). In short, the key shift brought about by structuralism was a focus on relations (in language, typically) rather than on things (as objects that can be named and known by humans).

For poststructuralists, the structuralist critique of humanism is correct – and to this extent all poststructuralists remain structuralists in important respects – but the tendency of structuralists to universalise the structures they unearthed 'behind phenomena' led them to being treated as surrogate humans; that is, there was a tendency within structuralism to impute a certain kind of agency to the structures themselves and place them at the centre of the world in an unchanging manner. Structuralism became, in the hands of some, a humanism of the background structure (though it is important to note that some recent interpretations of structuralism have maintained that this was always a concern of the structuralists that they were striving to overcome: see

Balibar 1997, 2005, and Maniglier 2005, 2006). In response, poststructuralists developed theoretical claims about the ways in which social structures change over time as well as how they differ in different contexts. Furthermore, they interrogated the idea of relationality at the heart of structuralism by considering what is required for a relation of difference (such as 'cat-dog-mouse') not to resolve itself into a relation of identity. These twin concerns gave rise to a new set of problems regarding the basis of social criticism – if structures change over time and difference is primary to identity then how are we to critique these structures when they seem to function in so many ways that restrict the proliferation of difference?

Post-foundationalism, on the other hand, draws from an alternative theoretical legacy. It is a term coined by Oliver Marchart (2007) to group a number of thinkers who share, he argues, a certain left-Heideggerian perspective: Jean-Luc Nancy, Claude Lefort, Ernesto Laclau and, one of the main thinkers to be discussed below, Alain Badiou. In short, left-Heideggerianism is a development of Heideggerian themes with a radical political agenda attached (Heidegger himself being thought to have had a philosophical position that was intrinsically problematic, conservative or quietist, depending on one's reading). In particular, the thinkers Marchart groups under this banner all develop Heidegger's conception of 'ontological difference' and turn it into a conception of 'political difference' (2007: 7). Indeed, Marchart concludes that political thought in the hands of these thinkers should be read as 'first philosophy' (2007: 162-9) borrowing a claim that Levinas (1989) makes about ethics. In the context of this discussion, one of the key notions shared by the post-foundationalists is that they all criticise the idea of necessary foundations while also claiming that all anti-foundationalist claims should be similarly critiqued. That is, they seek a form of social criticism that avoids both the dogmatism of necessary foundations and the scepticism of anti-foundational positions. The upshot is a series of related theoretical endeavours that all defend the *necessary contingency* of foundations. Given the importance of this idea, and the role it will play in the discussion below, it is worth briefly summarising what is at stake.

Heidegger (2000) was guided by one of the most basic questions of Western philosophy: why is there something rather than nothing? In a startling twist on the usual series of responses to this question, Heidegger dismissed all answers that began by pointing at or listing the things in the world, especially any attempt to list these in an order that would put some of them, atoms for example, as the primary things from which all others are constructed. But if these answers are insufficient for Heidegger then what is the meaning of the question at all? According to Heidegger it is a question that points not to the things or beings that make up the world, however we characterise these, but to *Being qua Being*. Being, in this sense, is not an entity of, or in the world; rather, it is that which marks out all entities as entities while not being an entity itself.

As helpfully summarised by Richard Polt: 'Being is the difference it makes that there is something rather than nothing' (1999: 3). So, how do we investigate or even ask the right questions about Being if we cannot begin with a list of beings? In the first instance, it is important, according to Heidegger, to note that the difference that there is something rather than nothing is especially related to time – as what is becomes what is not and what will be. Therefore, asking the right questions about Being requires us to investigate the temporality of beings. But how do we do this? His answer is deceptively simple: as we are beings who live in time, who are aware of our own sense of self, how it has changed and will change in the future, then we should turn to an investigation of ourselves, our being-in-time (Heidegger, 1962).

This is Heidegger's famous notion of Dasein: 'If to interpret the meaning of being becomes our task, Dasein is not only the primary entity to be interrogated; it is also that entity which already comports itself, in its Being, towards what we are asking about when we ask this question' (1962: 35). Like all such fundamental conceptual creations it has been subject to many different interpretations. Charles Taylor, however, gives a particularly useful gloss on what is meant by this term for our purposes. According to Taylor, we must always begin our investigations into nature, society, politics, culture and so on by first remembering that we are 'self-interpreting animals' (1985: 45). Indeed, we are the beings who are our interpretations of ourselves in all these respects. So, in search of Being, that which makes the difference that there is something rather than nothing, we must place many different interpretations of ourselves at the foundations of our investigations. That said, these foundations, because they are changeable interpretations, are always contingent upon our situation and, to this extent, never completely fixed foundations. This combination means that the foundations we seek when we ask about 'why this rather than that' are *necessary* because always present and inescapable but always *contingent* because never fixed or unchanging.

Already we can see that poststructuralists and post-foundationalists share a lot in common. They share the idea that how we make meaning in the world changes over time, that this brings a deep concern with difference to the fore and also that there is a sense in which we need to understand the grounds of meaningfulness, in structure in general and in the structures of Dasein in particular, but also that these grounds are never fixed and unchanging. In many respects, it is these deeply shared concerns that give rise to such interesting conceptualisations of the relationship between resistance, politics and truth in the thinkers associated with these positions. However, it is also clear that they are two positions that emerge from importantly different backgrounds – structuralism and Heidegger – and this gives distinctive textures to each of the positions that will become important. Initially, it raises questions regarding each position: is poststructuralism too deeply anti-humanist to provide the grounds for reformulating ways in which *our* practices of resistance may be sustained? Equally, is post-foundationalism too humanist to interrogate the consequences of humanist optimism that have led to new forms of domination? We will see that these questions about the nature of human cognition and practice, and how we should conceive of the conditions that shape these, will appear at several points in the discussion below; not least, in the opening foray between Chomsky and Foucault, but also throughout as we develop a critical conception of the relationship between resistance, politics and truth. By way of further scene-setting, though, and with an eye to specifying the detail of what is at stake in these discussions, it is worth taking one more step into analysing these two positions by considering the different ways in which they conceive of the relationship between politics and the political.

As characterised by Marchart (2007), post-foundational political thought is that which posits the political as the 'absent ground' of politics. As noted above, however, post-foundational political thinkers are best thought of, not as simple disciples of Heidegger (they all disagree with major elements of Heidegger's work, after all) but as 'left-Heideggerians'; thinkers deeply indebted to Heidegger's treatment of the ontological question and yet critical of the political quietism that his philosophy, particularly his later and more explicitly poetic work, entailed. In establishing this intricate relationship to Heidegger's thought, Marchart constructs a helpful framework for interpreting the thinkers that he situates within this post-foundational project. More than this, however, in establishing what he sees as the conceptual core of post-foundational political thought, Marchart is able to cast a (warmly) critical light on these thinkers. He argues that the post-foundational project can be described as the critique of the primacy of ontological difference from the perspective of the primacy of political difference. Ultimately, he argues, *the* political difference – that which exists between 'the political' and 'politics' should not be understood simply by analogy to the ontological difference; rather, 'ontological difference...has to be understood in the light of the political difference' (2007: 172). This leads Marchart to conclude that the Heideggerian project of articulating Being-qua-Being must be rethought as the project of establishing 'Being-qua-the political' (2007: 172); a project that leads to the startling claims that political thought is 'first philosophy' (2007: 162-69) and that *the* political difference (between politics and the political) should be understood *'as difference'*, in the Heideggerian sense.

It is important to draw out the distinction between this conception of the politics/political relationship with the version which animates poststructuralist political thought. In summary, poststructuralists argue that the political is best thought of as the open, rather than the absent, ground on which politics rests. Accepting, with Marchart, that traditional foundational gestures which enclose 'the political' are problematic and the claim that naïve anti-foundational gestures do more to uphold foundationalism than to challenge it, it is equally important to accept that the 'answer' to the question of how political thought moves beyond (anti-)foundationalism 'is, of course, the following: instead of an outright attack on foundationalism or "metaphysics", what should be attempted is the subversion of the very terrain on which foundationalism operates' (2007: 13). Furthermore, and as noted above, this internal subversion of foundations requires the careful elaboration of the *necessarily contingent* nature of all foundations. However, it is not the case for poststructuralists that this necessity and contingency must be articulated with reference to its alleged 'theoretical origin' in the work of Heidegger. Where Marchart employs Heidegger to unravel the absent yet productive ground that politics rests upon, I shall give a hint of what is to come below by employing Deleuze and Guattari's alternative subversion of metaphysics to support the claim that, as we will see, critical-political activity brings to life the political as the open ground that sustains it; a ground that, by virtue of being open, does not foreclose other critical interventions. In this respect, it is worth noting Michael Hardt's characterisation of Deleuze (and Guattari) as poststructuralist philosophers: 'Poststructuralism does critique a certain notion of foundation, but only to affirm another notion that is more adequate to its ends. Against a transcendental foundation we find an immanent one; against a given, teleological foundation we find a material, open one' (1983: vx). As we shall see, Hardt is right to characterise poststructuralism as a project concerned with the articulation of immanent foundations rather than as a project that is defined by trying to overcome the dyad of foundationalism and anti-foundationalism. This idea, of an immanent, material and open foundation, will serve as a guide on the journey to reposition the relationship between politics and the political away from Marchart's portrayal of 'left-Heideggerianism'.

With a view to specifying his characterisation of the post-foundational project in general and clarifying what is meant by the primacy of political difference, Marchart is drawn into some brief but important remarks about poststructuralism. From the very outset, poststructuralism is described 'as a term that reduces the genealogy of left Heideggerianism to the scientific paradigm of structuralism' (Marchart 2007: 2). Nonetheless, by the penultimate chapter on Laclau, Marchart appears to be uncritically accepting (approving may be too strong) Laclau's account of the importance of 'a more poststructuralist position' in the development of his own work on the difference between 'the social' and 'society' (2007: 135). This movement in the text is suggestive of a complicated set of assumptions on Marchart's behalf with regard to the relationship between post-foundationalism and poststructuralism. This complexity is indeed borne out by some of the comments made in the main body of the text.

The key discussion in this respect occurs as Marchart surveys 'the contours of left-Heideggerianism' (2007: chapter 1). Having raised the irrevocable nature of the 'questioning of grounds', Marchart then considers whether or not it makes sense to explain this questioning with relation to Heidegger's account of the gap between the ontic and the ontological given that 'poststructuralists... consider this difference redundant' (2007: 15). Is there a *necessity* to framing the relationship between politics and the political within a Heideggerian tradition? For Marchart, the answer is yes: 'if one has to accept *both* a plurality of contingent foundations which "empirically" – if always only temporarily – ground the social *and* the impossibility of a final ground for that plurality, it follows that this impossibility cannot be of the same order as the empirical foundations themselves' (2007: 15). Given this irreducible difference between the order of politics and the order of the political it would appear that all political theorists who invoke this distinction must indeed be (implicitly, at least) invoking Heidegger's account of the difference between the ontic world of beings and the ontological category of Being. This claim is substantiated with reference to 'the *locus classicus* of post-structuralism, Derrida's essay "Structure, Sign and Play in the Discourse of the Human Sciences"' (2007: 15). Rehearsing the arguments of this essay, Marchart concludes that we must accept, from the mouth of a poststructuralist (so to speak), that 'the impossibility of ground is a necessary impossibility', one that 'describes the necessary absence of an ultimate ground' albeit an absence that 'is a productive absence and not merely negative' (2007: 18). In two further references to the relationship between these two 'post-isms', Marchart initially presents poststructuralism alongside post-foundationalism as different theoretical positions that share a concern for contingency (2007: 26) and then later refers to 'a diverse and yet related set of theoretical approaches from "post-structuralism" or "left-Heideggerianism"' (2007: 61), implying, it would seem, a rather deeper bond between the two positions than merely a shared belief in the necessity of contingency (which is, as Marchart notes, also shared by most, if not all, post-isms) (2007: 26). There is, therefore, an ambiguity in Marchart's account of the relationship between post-foundationalism and poststructuralism. It is an ambiguity that runs deeper than being a result of the intrinsic slipperiness of classificatory approaches. This can be registered in the series of conceptual slippages from 'impossibility' to 'absence' to 'positive and negative' that marks out the conceptual terrain of the dispute with Marchart (and the left-Heideggerianism he characterises so adroitly). Before elaborating upon the nature of this dispute, however, it is important to speculate on the source of the ambiguity in Marchart's contextualisation of both post-foundationalism and poststructuralism.

Choosing Derrida's (1978) essay as the *locus classicus* of poststructuralism is legitimate to an extent, but not without its complications. It is immediately clear from reading Derrida that he takes Heidegger as one of his primary sources and influences; that he seeks to radicalise or move beyond his predecessor from a position of encampment within the field of Heidegger's thought. After all, Derrida's most notable neologism – deconstruction – emerges from and parallels in important ways Heidegger's idea of 'destruction' and his interpretation of Heidegger's ideas can be said, without doing too much violence to the texts, to be a thread that joins much of Derrida's diverse enquiries together. In short, to argue that poststructuralism is a form of post-foundationalism, on the basis that Derrida's contribution to the famous 1966 Johns Hopkins conference on structuralism positions what came to be known as poststructuralism within a Heideggerian conceptual and post-metaphysical landscape, is to verge on the tautologous. Derrida was already and remained Heideggerian in many important respects but his Heideggerian route into post-structuralism is far from the only one possible. A very different picture emerges if we consider the trajectory of another central figure of poststructuralism, and one central to this book; Deleuze.

John Protevi and Paul Patton put it well: '[w]hile it would be too simple to say that Derrida's notion of difference is essentially post-phenomenological and ethical and Deleuze's notion of difference is material and forceful, this characterisation does reflect real differences in their sources and philosophical orientations.' (2003: 5). There are two fundamental ways in which these real differences are manifest, fundamental that is in regard to the characterisation of the relationship between the post-foundational and the poststructuralist projects. First, Deleuze did not consider his work as informed (either negatively as critique or positively as influence) by Heidegger's historicisation of philosophy. For Deleuze, there was no need to be concerned with 'going beyond metaphysics or the death of philosophy' (1995: 88). For all that Deleuze and Guattari do indeed argue that philosophy was born in the particular conditions of ancient Greece, they do not accept that there is a necessity to this context or the form of its development (1994: 5). On the contrary, the philosophical task was always and will remain the task of constructing concepts. The effect of this a-historicist rendering of philosophical activity is to establish contingency on different grounds – grounds that are posited through the dramatization of concepts rather than as a result of the absence within them.

But there is a more profound matter at stake in thinking about Deleuze as a representative of poststructuralism. In Deleuze's work, especially in the work that is situated temporally at the emergence of poststructuralism (1966/7) and conceptually at the high watermark of his use of a 'method of dramatization', there is a claim to a form of 'absolute rationalism' (2004: 154); absolute by virtue of containing within it 'the concrete force of empiricism' (1992: 149). It is clear that these claims represent a markedly non-Heideggerian approach to the metaphysical tradition. Deleuze, in this respect, is a poststructuralist that views difference as empirically given in experience while also maintaining that it can be rationally justified as metaphysically prior to identity. It is clear that Deleuze prioritises difference in a way that does not rely upon the differentiation of the ontic and the ontological, at least not to posit any unassailable gap between the two. As such, to situate his work as part of a post-foundational project with its roots in Heidegger would be misleading, possibly erroneous. If we then also accept that the main themes of his work can be usefully characterised as poststructuralist then it is no longer possible to accept that poststructuralism is a version of post-foundationalism; and a 'reduced' version at that. It is a reductionism that Deleuze prefigured. For all that he recognised Heidegger as one of the 'great authors of our time' he cautioned against any approach to metaphysics that simply repeats 'a single question which would remain intact at the end, even if this question is "what is being?"' (Deleuze, 1994: 200). This is notwithstanding similar discussions of other poststructuralists, of course; though it is certainly plausible to claim that thinkers as diverse as Lyotard, Kristeva, Blanchot, Cixous or Foucault should not be treated as theorists that embody a post-foundational project, as described by Marchart (for example, see the essays collected in Dillet et al, 2013).

With what may appear to be rather parochial disagreement, what is at stake in basing a poststructuralist understanding of the relationship between politics and the political on Deleuze and Guattari's subversion of metaphysics rather than on Heidegger's? In short, the post-foundational politicization of Heidegger's ontological difference does not in fact, despite claims to the contrary, avoid the sceptical quietism that beset Heidegger's project or, to the extent that it does, it becomes dogmatic. We can see this in the ways in which contemporary left-Heideggerianism foregrounds an 'irruptive' conception of politics that issues from their post-foundational conceptualisations of the political, a conception that either leads one to say that nothing is at stake in our everyday world of resistance and politics or that everything is at stake (if it is a truly irruptive moment, as we will see in the work of Badiou). For all that this is an event-oriented conception of how resistance, politics and truth may be related, ultimately the post-foundationalist position cannot sustain the evental dimensions of a *critical* account of the relationship between politics and the political because such 'irruptivism' is unable to sustain an idea of critique itself. The 'absent ground' of the political is no ground at all on which to base critique; if, as will be argued below, critique is conceived as the production of difference and, therefore, as the overcoming of indifference. The 'left-Heideggerians', for all that they challenge Heidegger's ideas, therefore remain trapped within his historicist ambit and his poetic appeal to moments of rupture. Whereas Marchart claims that 'event, moment, freedom and difference' need to be recovered from within Heidegger's work in order to 'subvert' the foundationalist position rather than being implicated in logics of denial that inevitably end up supporting the foundationalist claims, one of the failures of these post-foundationalist thinkers is a failure to grasp the nature of critical-political events as the expression of a radically aesthetic form of critique (even though it is important to acknowledge that all the left-Heideggerians make substantial in-roads into both the nature of events and of aesthetic critique). Bringing the political to life, through creative practices and resistant acts, requires positing it as the 'open ground' upon which critique can multiply as a series of events; where events are understood aesthetically, that is, as the creation of difference in a world where the clamour of criticism leads to indifference.

For the moment, it is important to hold this claim, as it will become justified as the discussion unfolds and weaves through the major thinkers to be considered below. In this discussion, this difference between poststructuralist and post-foundationalist conceptions of grounding will be explored through the construction of a series of debates and discussions between Foucault, Deleuze and Badiou. We will come to appreciate some of the major themes – humanism, anti-humanism, foundationalism, anti-foundationalism, necessity and contingency, event, critique and art – from within the detailed interpretations of each of the thinkers and the textual focus that will shape the following chapters. However, framing this discussion with Marchart's help, as one between rival conceptions of an evental relationship between resistance, politics and truth, situates these detailed discussions in a more general manner; thereby opening up further work that could be done on the complicated interlocking of these two positions in thinkers such as Laclau and Ranciere, among others.

The debates begin, however, where the general characterisation of these two positions began; with rival versions of humanism and structuralism. Through a reading of the Chomsky/Foucault debate on human nature and power in the next chapter, it will be claimed that we can no longer presume the truth about human nature and our political situation and that, instead, we must begin with the idea that truths, including those about our nature as human beings, are irreducibly political. The question this poses is whether or not we can then hope to have forms of resistance to oppressive regimes, of whatever kind, without assuming that we know the truth about politics; a question that dominates the second half of their famous discussion. In chapter two, it will be argued that Foucault provides resources for a positive answer to this question through a) his analysis of institutions and b) his work on the techniques of the self. Nonetheless, it will be shown that Foucault's position is open to criticism because it does not have the philosophical resources within itself to ground the position he stakes out. These philosophical resources are explored through the work of Deleuze, in chapter three. Deleuze provides a way of thinking about thought that is aimed at rooting out all forms of dogmatism and scepticism. At the crux of his account is the idea of learning through an encounter with the outside and this will be explored in depth. However, it is notable that there is little room for any talk of truth in Deleuze's alternative image of thought. This is indeed one of the reasons that Badiou has been so critical of Deleuze, as we will see in chapter four: Deleuze's philosophical presuppositions seem to rob thought of any radical impact and jeopardise forms of political resistance. Badiou's alternative will be explored, focussing on the evental nature of truth and how he conceives of the formation of militant political subjects. The last chapter will conclude, however, that Badiou's position does not avoid the dogmatism that will always have resistance run aground on the shores of capitalism whereas a reconfigured version of Foucault/Deleuze (one that takes the critical dimension of their work seriously, i.e. in a way that disables Badiou's criticism) can ground forms of resistance as the art of events. In the conclusion, I will return to the idea of what this critically oriented version of poststructuralism offers for new ways of thinking and acting in our world, today.

For those approaching this text looking for insights into particular forms of resistance the journey just outlined may seem impoverished by virtue of its academicism, its overtly theoretical tone. It is a justifiable concern. However, it is time for a proper interrogation of what is at stake between forms of poststructuralism and post-foundationalism from a political point of view with a focus on resistance not least because we live in times when new forms of protest have caught many commentators in the social movement literature unaware. Many of the forms of resistance that have characterised so much of political life since the global financial crisis of 2008, including the so-called but misnamed 'Arab-Spring', require new forms of theorisation that shift the terms away from pre-established conceptions of what counts as political action (be it in terms of interest, class or identity) in order to give a better understanding of what happens in these practices of resistance. Most of the literature in this area treats practices of resistance as objects of study within traditional social science research. There is very little that tackles the tricky question of how theory and practice relate: how consistently articulated practices may become sustainable forms of resistance. Shifting our critical attention toward these two event-oriented theories opens up the discussion in ways that bring creative practices and resistant acts into view, without reifying either but empowering both (Hussein/MacKenzie, 2017). Although it is ultimately beyond the scope of this text, there is a lingering question that is important to foreground as we travel through the intricacies of the theoretical discussion below: can we bring new *practices* of resistance into dialogue with *new ways of thinking* about what happens when we resist in mutually sustaining ways?

At the heart of this problem is what we mean by politics and the political and how we conceive of their relation to truth and resistance. The establishing gambit is that focussing on what happens in resistance moves us on from either dogmatic or sceptical debates about what interests are at stake, what class position is being mobilised or what identities are being voiced. Thinking and acting differently in the world, in ways that empower practices of resistance against complex regimes that oppress and dominate our lives, while also avoiding both dogmatism and scepticism with regard to the mutual implication of power, politics and truth, requires a creative practice of learning as the basis of true critique. We require new forms of practice to enable new ways of thinking about our situation and what we may change about it, but we also require modes of thinking in order to establish practices that will bring these changes into existence. In the relay between theory and practice, at the interstice of politics and the open ground of the political, we find ways of conceptualising and expressing the events that can shake the status quo and the ways to sustain them against the tendency toward recuperation within the very regimes we find so disempowering. It may not be as simple as hoping that 'the truth will set us free' but neither is it as defeatist as to think that 'the truth will always be on the side of those in power'. In creative practices and resistant acts there is an evental relationship between politics, truth and resistance that is expressed through the artistry of making a significant and lasting (or, one could say, critical) difference, in a political world that seems all too comfortable, even in its alleged radical forms, with contemporary forms of indifference. To think and act differently in the world today is to overcome the indifference brought about by both dogmatic simplicity and sceptical defeatism by treating critique, in both theory and practice, as a creative practice of, and a resistant act guided by, learning.

# Chapter 1: From the Truth about Politics to the Politics of Truth

In the Introduction, the themes that will guide this discussion were framed with reference to the similarities and differences between poststructuralist and post-foundationalist political theory. This chapter will develop and increasingly specify the key questions within these themes that will guide the rest of the book. It will focus on the famous exchange between Chomsky and Foucault in 1971 as this helps establish what is at stake when one invokes truth in the name of resistance (Chomsky) and when one suspends the category of truth in order to subject it to a political analysis while remaining committed to resistance (Foucault). The stakes of this debate could not have been higher. It was a time of great political upheaval as well as national and international conflict: the waves of unrest that characterised the civil rights movements and the conflict in Vietnam being the most obvious contexts framing this discussion between two emergent public intellectuals of global significance. Although this exchange begins with what seems like a rather arcane discussion of the nature of scientific claims, this does help to establish the difference between Chomsky's naturalism and radical humanism and the poststructuralist scepticism regarding both of these terms underpinning Foucault's account of knowledge. As such, the terms are set for what becomes an increasingly clear political dispute between the two activist philosophers. Tracing this dispute we come to appreciate the importance of the differing accounts they give of the relationship between language and creativity and the way this frames their discussions of the idea of human nature and a range of more straightforwardly political matters such as the different ways they view the relationship between justice and power. Furthermore, the differences between the two positions become ever clearer and the stakes of the questions that emerge ever more pronounced. As we will see, this also enables us to define both the structuralism that guides Foucault's version of a poststructuralist position and, in a certain sense, its similarity to the humanism that animates Chomsky's. Nonetheless, the political implications of Foucault's poststructuralist claims become more evident as the challenge to Chomsky's humanism is developed through their conversation. The chapter will end with a clear statement of what it means to bring 'the politics of truth' centre stage in our philosophies of resistance, with a first hint of why it is important to focus on *what happens* in practices of resistance.

### What's science got to do with it?

In the modern world, when we think about how we are guided by the truth in our practices of resistance, it is commonplace to look to science for the claims that can count as true. Although there are many forms of naturalism (the idea that the natural sciences provide the best available methods and conclusions for claims about nature and our nature as human beings) the general pervasiveness of this position is evident in social, cultural, economic, political and philosophical debates to this day. Furthermore, that naturalism and humanism emerged at similar historical periods, in the epochs of the Renaissance and the early modern development of the inductive scientific method, indicates a deep connection between these two positions. Even if, strictly speaking, they are not the same thing – one can be a humanist without being a naturalist and vice-versa – it is evident that when we are motivated to resist by the idea that 'the truth will set us free' it is often scientific truths that shape what we have in mind, and that give us the courage to think that the false claims of convention and ideology will, in the end, be overcome just as surely as the Medieval lies about women deemed to be witches, for example, were similarly overcome. Of course, we also know that scientific claims have been subject to rigorous critique from those who see it as a discipline intimately bound to money, power and state militarism. So, naturalists have to articulate their claims with an awareness of how to distinguish the importance of the method over the conclusions, lest they be tainted by convention and ideology, as well as a way of separating the integrity of scientific claims from those claims that have emerged from within science that have since been shown to be not just false but dangerous, even disastrous (such as the scientific claims about racial eugenics that emerged from within the Nazi regime). If one wants to motivate one's practices of resistance with claims that are both naturalist and humanist, therefore, it is important to be subtle and reflective about exactly what claims one is defending and why. We see this subtlety and reflexivity in the way that Chomsky approaches the discussion with Foucault, especially with regard to the concept of 'human nature'. In setting up the discussion, and introducing Chomsky, the mediator, Fons Elders, neatly establishes the problem when he says:

All studies of man, from history to linguistics and psychology, are faced with the question of whether, in the last instance, we are the product of external factors, or if, in spite of our differences, we have something we could call a common human nature, by which we can recognise each other as human beings...Which arguments can you [Chomsky] derive from linguistics to give such a central position to this concept of human nature? (2006: 2).

Chomsky's opening foray in the discussion in response to this question presents just the kind of subtle naturalism and humanism that is often at stake in contemporary forms of radical positions that defend the importance of our need to resist structures of oppression and domination in the name of truth.

In establishing his vision of human nature, Chomsky is keen to acknowledge that the scientific concepts 'presently available to us' do not necessarily give him hope with regard to a full and rich understanding of human cognitive capacities – our capacity to know the world and to reflect on our knowledge of the world (2006: 8). Rather, scientists will have to 'broaden their scope' in order to investigate, without prejudice, the nature of human cognition. Nonetheless, this cautious naturalism is still a form of naturalism, to the extent that Chomsky is pinning his methodological hopes on the natural sciences to provide such a theory of human cognition. This becomes clear when he says that one of the tasks of this broad vision of science is to bring the rigors of science to bear not just on the interaction of bodies – be they human, physical or cosmological – but on the mind. It is with this spirit that he speculates that it is possible, in principle at least, and necessary from a methodological point of view, to get behind 'the task of carrying on and developing [a] mathematical theory of mind' (2006: 13). By which he means: 'a precisely articulated, clearly formulated, abstract theory which will have empirical consequences, which will let us know whether the theory is right or wrong, or on the wrong track or the right track' (2006: 13). This last qualification is important. Subtle and reflective forms of naturalism and humanism must accept that sometimes scientists get it wrong or are on the wrong track, but behind this claim is the idea that it is only scientific method that will enable us to know whether or not this is the case. For all this caution, though, we see Chomsky's position harden as the conversation develops. As he defends the role of science in establishing naturalist claims about human cognition, and in doing so acknowledges that the prospect of a complete accommodation of a science of human cognition within the natural sciences as they currently exist is a long way off in the future, he remains steadfast with regard to the possibility of such a unified science of what we know and how we know what we know about the world. Indeed, for Chomsky, it is 'the fact that science converges and progresses', a fact he deems established by the historical development of the disciplines of the natural sciences, that gives him this optimism that naturalism and humanism will combine forces in a science of human creativity with real political clout. We will dwell on the substance of this optimism, Chomsky's empirical and theoretical investigations into the nature of language and creativity, in the next section. It is important to establish first, though, that Foucault takes a different view of scientific development and progress because this helps frame the substantive dispute between them and the political positions that emerge later in the conversation.

When he is invited by Elders to respond to Chomsky's view of scientific progress with the presumption that he will have 'severe criticism of this', Foucault initially suggests that 'there are one or two little historical points' that he would like to add. In fact, these 'little historical points' turn out to be precursors to a rather major difference in the way that Foucault views science and the idea of progress that animates it; generally, and for Chomsky. The 'little historical points' amount to interpretive dispute about which of the seventeenth and eighteenth century rationalists are closer to Chomsky's position; Leibniz and Pascal, rather than Descartes, according to Foucault. However, as Elders presses him on his historical understanding of science, Foucault begins to give a more pertinent set of responses. While both Chomsky and Foucault acknowledge that the truths produced by science have changed over time, even since the modern period and the development of scientific method, it is notable that Foucault does not situate those changes within the methodological apparatus itself. For Foucault, the problem with assuming that its method defines what we think of as science is that the scientific method itself presumes both 'the principle of the sovereignty of the subject' and that 'the historical dimension of knowledge is always negative in relation to truth' (2006: 16). In the first of these presumptions there is, for Foucault, a tendency to overplay the originality of the great scientific inventor; over and above, that is, the conditions that make such invention possible. Although he doesn't put it exactly like this, Foucault is, in effect, casting doubt on what we might call a 'great man' theory of historical change when imported into the history of science. The beginnings of his sceptical attitude to humanism are, as such, already evident. The second presumption, that truth and the history of scientific development stand in a negative relation to each other, casts doubt on the role that distancing scientific knowledge from convention and traditional forms of knowledge constitutes a, perhaps, unwarranted guarantee of the idea of scientific progress as embedded within the idea of scientific method. Rather than presume such things, that science progresses through the 'eccentric' intervention of great scientists in traditional fields of knowledge, he argues that we should 'superimpose' the history of scientific development with that of the history of the idea of the subject and of progress (so as not to presume both the subject and progress and then separate them out from the development of the sciences themselves).

Taking as an example medicine at the end of the eighteenth century, Foucault says it would be 'artificial' to attribute the developments made at this time to any one individual just as it would be a mistake to attribute these to the negation of traditional medicinal routines. Rather, he says that these transformations were the result 'of a collective and complex transformation of medical understanding in its practices and rules' (2006: 18). Such collective and complex transformation cannot, for Foucault, either simply be attributed to individuals applying proper scientific method or to the ways in which they distanced themselves from their immediate past. Rather, for Foucault, his historical approach to the changing truths of science makes him attentive to the analysis of the conditions that account for the ways in which 'the understanding modifies itself in its formative rules, without passing through an original "inventor" discovering the "truth"' (2006: 18).

Although Foucault initially attributes this difference in perspective to 'the state of the disciplines', linguistics and history respectively (2006: 19, 32-33), by the time Chomsky's declared belief in scientific progress has come to the fore Foucault is adopting a rather more critical stance. He says:

> For a long time the idea has existed that the sciences, knowledge, followed a certain 'progress', obeying the principle of 'growth', and the principle of the convergence of all these kinds of knowledge. And yet when one sees how the European understanding, which turned out to be a worldwide and universal understanding in a historical and geographical sense, developed, can one say that there has been growth? I, myself, would say that it has been much more a matter of transformation. (2006: 26)

Not only is Foucault challenging by this point the very idea of an, in principle, convergence of the sciences of bodies (what we know about the world) and of minds (how we know what we know about the world), he is also demonstrating his fundamental suspicion of the very idea of such convergence being treated as the hallmark of progress. Preferring the more neutral term, transformation, Foucault is already raising doubts about the value of pinning our hopes on science for the truths that will set us free. Chomsky's avowed hope that one day the natural sciences will give a full and deep account of the cognitive faculties that allow us to know the world as human beings and that such progress is built into the scientific method is met with Foucault's rather more historical view that the best one can say is that knowledge, the practices, routines and rituals that sustain it, have transformed over time, without being able to say for sure whether or not we can call this progress.

It is worth pausing to sum up what this has to do with our guiding themes about resistance, politics and truth. In this opening exchange between Chomsky and Foucault we see the crux of the debates between humanism and poststructuralism. Humanists tend to ally themselves with naturalism and the scientific method to the extent that this method puts human beings, as subjects that come to know the world and thereby give it meaning, at the centre of things. For the poststructuralist, the rules and systems underlying the production of knowledge are more important such that the knowing subject is displaced from centre stage and the changes to the systems of rules become paramount.

The key epistemological but also political question that emerges is whether or not we can rely on the sciences to bring about if not the truth then progressively better, more truthful, understandings of the world and our place in it. Chomsky, without naivety, pins his hopes on this view of scientific progress, whereas Foucault's historical investigations have made him wary of placing too much emphasis on this idea. If we moderns tend to look to science, therefore, as the source of the truths that will set us free then it is usually done so in the name of social and political progress. Indeed, it is hard to imagine practices of resistance that do not avow such an ideal (though one can think of conservative forms of resistance that seek to maintain the status quo). What happens to our idea of resistance if we give up progress? If we accept Foucault's more cautious rendering of the 'transformations' wrought by science then are we already robbing ourselves of that which motivates us to resist in the first place: that the truth will set us free and therefore the world will be a better place? It is important to specify these questions early in the discussion because they will return throughout, even up to the particular version of a mathematically articulated set of precise claims animating Badiou's theory of the militant subject and its fidelity to truth (Chapter 4). However, at this stage it is important to specify the substance of the opening debate between Chomsky and Foucault, as this takes us closer to the philosophical stakes of their dispute. As we will see, it is not just a dispute between scientific method and the history of the sciences but one about the sources of human creativity, especially vis-à-vis language.

## Language and Creativity

We noted in the Introduction that structuralists tend to treat language as a set of relations that generate meaning rather than focus on human intentionality. This is not to say that humanists have not been concerned with the nature of language, or that they haven't developed sophisticated accounts of the structures that impinge on human intentionality; far from it. In the debate between Chomsky and Foucault, in fact, we see how a subtle account of linguistic creativity is given a humanist twist by Chomsky. But we also see how Foucault situates this creativity outside of the human in a manner that gives his poststructuralist emphasis on transformation a distinctly structuralist basis.

Perhaps Chomsky's most innovative theoretical claim is that there is a universal grammar underpinning all known languages (see, for example, Chomsky 1965 and 1968). In this discussion with Foucault, he gives a particularly lucid account of how he came to this position and, as we will see, how it motivates a radically oriented set of social and political claims for which he has become equally well known (see, for example, Chomsky 2008, for a text that brings together his key texts in linguistics and politics). His interest in linguistics started with 'a very definite empirical problem' (2006: 2): it is clear that competent language users have a capacity for the highly creative use of their language(s). As he says, 'much of what a person says in his normal intercourse with others is novel, much of what you hear is new...in fact, it has much of the characteristics of what I think might very well be called creativity' (2006: 2). Nonetheless, it is equally clear, for Chomsky, that in the midst of such creativity it remains true that speakers of the same language can, mostly, understand one another. 'There is only one possible explanation', he says, 'namely, the assumption that the individual contributes a good deal' to both creative language use and to being able to understand the creative language use of others (2006: 3). Given the great diversity of language use and understanding, this contribution of the individual must be instinctive or innate. As he concludes his opening summary, 'I would claim then that this instinctive knowledge, if you like, this schematism that makes it possible to derive complex and intricate knowledge on the basis of very partial data, is one fundamental constituent of human nature' (2006: 4).

Chomsky's use of the term 'schematism' is particularly instructive. Later on in the discussion he gives a succinct version of what he means by this: it is 'the concept of free creation within a system of rule' (2006: 12). In both instances, it is impossible not to hear the Kantian overtones of this claim; even though in this context Chomsky does not make this link explicit. In Kant, schematism is a cognitive procedure by which the categories of the understanding are linked to empirical sensations as presented to the understanding through the intuition (1998: 271-277). Without delving too deeply into the interpretive quagmire surrounding this term, the Kantian vision of human cognition treats all sensation as filtered, first, through the intuition that organises our sensations in space and time and then, second, as categorised by the twelve abstract concepts of the understanding (causality, modality, quality, quantity, etc). In a further act of imagination, the knowing subject then schematises the intuited experience with their placement in the categories of the understanding to produce knowledge of the world. As Caygill defines it, the schematism 'is a procedure of the judgement which adapts otherwise heterogeneous concepts to the spatial and temporal conditions of intuition' (1995: 360). Explaining this (rather loosely, admittedly), one can say, for example, that the thing I perceive here and now in front of me on the mat, has the quality of fluffiness, four legs, makes a meowing sound etc and when joined together, my experience of the thing and how it fits with my understanding requires me to combine, schematically, the two aspects together to know that it is, in fact, a cat sitting on the mat. What is instructive for us, in this discussion, is that Chomsky embraces Kant's 'Copernican revolution' (1998: 110) and treats the human capacity for creative language use and understanding as a product of our innate cognitive structures. In language we can creatively explore what it is that joins our sense experience to our understanding of that experience – coming up with new words and images for the cat on the mat – but we do so within a system of rules that means we understand each other when our interlocutor is similarly creative. In essence, as Chomsky puts it, 'the structure of the knowledge that is acquired in the case of language is basically internal to the human mind' (2006: 24).

Where one might be tempted to say that such human creativity situated within the human mind is beyond the reach of science, we have already noted that Chomsky takes a different view: 'now my belief is that science can look forward to the problem of normal creativity as a topic that it can perhaps incorporate within itself' (2006: 20). It is worth pausing on this statement. The 'normal creativity' alluded to here is his way of distinguishing the claim he wishes to make from what he thinks Foucault is saying about the rare creative moments when the sciences transform their rules and systems. So, at one level, he is adopting Foucault's view that their differing approaches may be a matter of the different disciplines to which they are seeking to contribute. However, the more crucial point is that Chomsky once again demonstrates his commitment to a unified view of the sciences; one that can bring the physics of bodily movement into alignment with a science of our cognition, at least to the extent that language is central to cognition. The source he draws upon is Kant and, in effect, he is arguing that, one day (and, again, the caution Chomsky displays about the current state of the natural sciences means that he is no evangelist about science as it stands) we will have a naturalist view of Kant's schematism to 'incorporate' how we know the world into a view of what we know about the world, through the scientific method. This is a rich and compelling vision. It is not a vision of the scientific reduction of our creativity to merely deterministic laws of causality, but a vision of how science can help us better understand our capacities as creative language users without diminishing that capacity, in anyway.

As already noted in the Introduction, and as an issue that will come to the fore as we develop the differences between a poststructuralist and a post-foundationalist position, one of the questions that haunts any (post)structuralist account is that of whether or not it can properly account for human agency, especially in practices of resistance. We will see in later chapters how the idea of creativity will come centre stage, in the work of Deleuze especially, but it is important at this moment to take a little time to spell out the similarities and differences between Foucault and Chomsky on this issue. Initially, Foucault describes creativity in terms similar to Chomsky: 'one can only, in terms of language or of knowledge, produce something new by putting into play a certain number of rules which will define the acceptability or grammaticality of these statements' (2006: 22). In this sense, neither Foucault nor Chomsky are appealing to a Romantic ideal of spontaneous creation as an act of individual will, at least to the extent that they both recognise the dialectic between rule and creation. However, a crucial difference emerges when one considers where these rules are situated for each thinker.

We have just noted that for Chomsky they are situated in 'the human mind'. Foucault takes a rather different approach. If we return to his example of changes in medicine in the eighteenth century then we can see that the rules and systems that make certain new statements about the human body possible, according to Foucault, are best represented as 'the application of an entirely new *grille* [grid]' (2006: 18). This grid is the system of regularities that make new statements possible. And, as he says later, 'where I don't completely agree with Mr Chomsky is when he places the principle of these regularities, in a way, in the interior of the mind or of human nature' (2006: 29). For Foucault, placing the rules and regularities inside the human mind simply reproduces the idea of the sovereign subject that similarly underpins the idea of a progressive scientific method: in fact, this move, therefore, is the basis of Chomsky's combined vision of naturalism and humanism, a vision that Foucault's more historical investigations has called into question to the extent that the sovereign subject itself is a historical invention rather than a universal claim about our innate cognitive capacities. He sums up his concerns and his alternative view of how to situate these rules and regularities as follows:

...to say that these regularities are connected, as conditions of existence, to the human mind or its nature is difficult for me to accept: it seems to me that one must, before reaching that point – and in any case I am only talking about the understanding – replace it in the field of other human practices, such as economics, technology, politics, sociology, which can serve them as conditions of formation, of models, of place, of apparition etc. I would like to know whether one cannot discover the system of regularity, of constraint, which makes science possible, even outside the human mind, in social forms, in relations of production, in the class struggles etc. (2006: 29)

Although this is a rich quote that speaks to Foucault's archaeological investigations up to this point, it's key feature for us is that he locates the schematism that enables new statements to be produced outside of the human mind in a variety of different, indeed overlapping, formations. But we must be clear on what this means. It does not mean that Foucault is simply rejecting the Kantian elements of Chomsky's version of linguistic creativity. Rather, it means that he is accepting the general idea that new statements emerge from within the application of rules and regularities in imaginative ways but that the source of such creativity is not to be located within the mind rather within the collective structures of such rules and regularities. In this sense, we get a good view of Foucault's structuralism and its centrality to his poststructuralist position with regard to the changing rules and regularities of science and knowledge more generally. Of course, without the poststructuralist emphasis upon the changing systems of knowledge we can see how easily structuralism can become a form of humanism; one that simply adopts the Kantian framework of timeless rules and regularities (categories of the understanding) in the pursuit of a 'deeper and broader' science of the human. However, one can also see how important structuralism is to poststructuralism, despite some attempts to characterise the 'post' as an 'anti', and to this extent retain the idea that poststructuralism is deeply wedded to the Kantian project of finding the conditions for the production of legitimate forms of knowledge. What both aspects bring to the fore, and this will become ever more evident as the discussion unfolds below, is that it is clear that poststructuralism is a critical philosophy, one that is indebted to Kant and the task of critically interrogating all claims to knowledge from the point of view of their conditions (for a rich discussion of this critical inheritance see, Han: 2002). This critical dimension in itself does not provide the full response to the problem of agency that besets (post)structuralist accounts (that will come in the next chapter as we develop Foucault's more positive version of critical theory as a practice of resistance) but it does already suggest that it would be too quick simply to dismiss poststructuralism as uncritical on account of its emphasis upon structure rather than agency. We can refine this a little further by examining Chomsky's and Foucault's competing accounts of the status of the concept of human nature itself.

## Human Nature at the Limit

We have seen, so far, the importance of several key claims when it comes to articulating the similarities and differences between Chomsky and Foucault: first and foremost there is the difference between Chomsky's naturalist and humanist account of the possibility for a unified science of what we know and how we know what we know about the world from Foucault's historical investigations that treat the development of the sciences and the development of ideas of the sovereign human subject as correlated, 'superimposed', historical phenomena rather than universal features of reasonable method. In addition, we have noted that both thinkers place a high value on creativity, understood as a process that is intimately bound up with the rules and regularities that enable knowledge of the world, but that they do so in different ways to the extent that Chomsky sees these regularities as an innate feature of human cognition whereas Foucault situates them in the world outside the human mind. When it comes to thinking about what these competing approaches mean with regard to human nature it is rather easier to see what is at stake for Chomsky than for Foucault.

For Chomsky, what he discerns about our ability as creative language users – that we are able to manipulate language in incredibly creative ways while also being able to understand each other – points to a more general claim; 'in other domains of human cognition and behaviour, something of the same sort must be true' (2006: 4). Our capacity for linguistic creativity, therefore, is a marker for our general capacity as creative human beings in all areas of 'thought and interaction' (2006: 4). He says, 'this mass of schematisms, innate organising principles, which guides our social and intellectual and individual behaviour, that's what I mean to refer to by the concept of human nature' (2006: 4-5). Given the previous discussions, we can see both the cautious optimism of Chomsky's naturalism and his commitment to humanism of a broadly Kantian variety. Moreover, talking about the ways in which a child acquires the ability to understand complex language systems and use them creatively, he says 'there is something biologically given, unchangeable, a foundation for whatever it is that we do with our mental capacities in this case' (2006: 7). It all adds up to a wonderfully clear, but subtle, articulation of the links between naturalism, humanism and foundationalism. An account of our human nature must serve as the foundation for all further investigations of human interaction and this nature can be accessed, in principle if not yet in practice, through the natural sciences. The 'next peak to scale' for the natural sciences is a fully worked out theory, one that is precisely formulated but subject to empirical verification, of these features that are common to our humanity as creative beings. Interestingly, he adds, as biologists have 'already answered to the satisfaction of some the question of what is life' they should now turn their attention to answering the following question: how do we know that we are beings capable of knowing the world and provide answers about our cognitive capacities that fit together with our already existing scientific accounts of living organisms?

However, this reference to the question of 'life' in biology is not as straightforward as Chomsky thinks, at least according to Foucault. Beginning rather tentatively, Foucault states that not all the concepts used within the sciences have neither the same 'degree of elaboration' nor the same function. In biology, there are concepts, he says, that are primarily classificatory, allowing scientists to group different phenomena, while others function to 'fix relations' between or as biological mechanisms, such as the concept of reflex. But the concepts that particularly interest Foucault, as a historian of how the sciences have changed their objects of study over time, are those that function on the periphery of the science, in this case biology. Such peripheral concepts play a crucial role as they are the concepts 'by which scientific practice designates itself, differentiates itself in relation to other practices, delimits its domain of objects, and designates what it considers to be the totality of its future tasks' (2006: 5-6). In the case of biology, the concept of 'life' is one such concept, though he adds immediately 'during a certain period' (2006: 6). According to Foucault it was only by the end of the eighteenth century that the concept of life assumed the role of organising the new array of other concepts brought into existence in part by new technologies and by new practices of investigation. In this sense, Foucault says that 'life' is not a scientific concept, rather it is an 'epistemological indicator' (2006: 6).

What does Foucault mean by this? Whereas the concept of 'tissue' designates parts of the human body in ways that enable us to know something about it in scientific terms, the concept of life does not in itself designate anything; rather, it 'indicates' the legitimate set of objects that can be known biologically. In this sense, life is not something that can be known scientifically, as it is precisely the concept that allows and enables other things to be known about living organisms; life itself is unknowable. Moreover, given Foucault's insistence on the historical emergence of this organising concept, it is clear that he thinks it is an indicator of what can be known 'during a certain period' rather than a concept that allows us to know once and for all, so to speak, what counts as legitimate knowledge in the domain of biology. In other words, the sciences are defined in large measure by their employment of such epistemological indicators but given that these change over time so the matter of what counts as legitimate within the sciences – legitimate technologies, practices and objects of knowledge – change over time. Crucially, such changes are not driven by ever more acute methodological claims but by a whole array of economic, social, political and cultural changes with which they are deeply embroiled. We are once again drawn to Foucault's idea that we must remain suspicious about all claims that rely upon the presumption of scientific progress and focus instead upon the ways in which the sciences have transformed over time without assuming that these transformations are necessarily bringing us closer to the truth about what we know and how we know what we know.

With this idea of an epistemological indicator presented in general, Foucault is well equipped to make his view about the idea of human nature clear:

Well, it seems to me that the notion of human nature is of the same type. It was not by studying human nature that linguists discovered the laws of constant mutation, or Freud the principles of the analysis of dreams, or cultural anthropologists the structure of myths. In the history of knowledge, the notion of human nature seems to me to have played the role of an epistemological indicator to designate certain types of discourse in relation to or in opposition to theology or biology or history. I would find it difficult to see in this a scientific concept. (2006: 6-7)

Whereas Chomsky understands the concept of life to be at the centre of biology and the concept of human nature to be at the centre of a newly configured science of human cognition, Foucault treats both concepts as indicators of the limits of certain domains that have emerged since the eighteenth century because of a wide array of changes, yes within the sciences, but also within economics, society and politics. Functioning at the limit, human nature is not something that can be known simply because it is that which allows other features of human interaction to become objects of knowledge. However, we must be careful in our elaboration of this idea of human nature as a limit concept, as an epistemological indicator.

It is tempting to assume that if one does not embrace a fully-fledged account of human nature, such as Chomsky's, then one must be an anti-humanist. This is true only to a certain extent; that is, to the extent that Foucault does not feel able to embrace the idea that the human capacity for knowledge about the world will also turn in on itself and become a human centred account of how we humans come to know the world (thereby placing the human at the centre of all knowledge). But caution about this grand humanist vision does not amount to dismissing the idea of human nature altogether; in fact, Foucault's idea of it as an epistemological indicator places it at the forefront of his analyses into the changing practices, rules and regularities of the sciences of 'man'. That he concluded in these investigations that man was about to be 'erased, like a face drawn in sand at the edge of the sea' (Foucault, 2002a: 422), that is that the human sciences were on the verge of becoming differently organised, does not in itself mean that there is little or no value on the idea of human nature as a diagnostic for this transformation; indeed, he quickly dismisses Elders' suggestion that this is the case (2006: 30). And, furthermore, it does not mean that he necessarily underestimates the role of human creativity in his analyses of the sciences or, as we will see below, in politics. Rather, his claim is more subtle than has sometimes been presented: he sees human creativity as conditioned in ways that do not simply situate those conditions within the human mind, as universal features of our cognitive abilities. The point is that for Foucault, human nature functions as a concept to delimit disciplines from each other and as such it is to be investigated with a focus on 'the society in which we live, the economic relations within which it functions, and the system of power which defines the regular forms and the regular permissions and prohibitions of our conduct' (2006: 37). In this sense, he says, 'the essence of our life consists, after all, of the political functioning of the society in which we find ourselves' (2006: 37).

There is a certain paradoxical quality to this last statement. On the one hand, it has the hallmark of a foundationalist claim – it is a claim about the essence of our life. On the other hand, this essence is expressed historically, that is it changes over time depending on our social, economic and political formations. It is here that we see Foucault embrace the major developments of post-Kantian thought as expressed in Hegel and Marx. Our cognitive features as human beings are inextricably linked to our historical situation, which in itself is linked to our social, economic and political regimes. However, we will see in the remaining two sections of this chapter that Foucault remains suspicious of the political implications of embracing this idea alongside the progressive politics that both Hegel and Marx embraced, while Chomsky takes a certain version of Marxism and hooks it firmly to his universal account of human nature and his naturalism. It is a distinction between the two positions that was already prefigured by Foucault in the opening forays about science, creativity, life and human nature:

> You will say to me that all the Marxist historians of science have been doing this for a long time. But when one sees how they work with these facts and especially what use they make of the notions of consciousness, of ideology as opposed to science, one realizes that they are for the main part more or less detached from the theory of knowledge. (2006: 17)

This theme of 'detachment', of the ways in which naturalist and humanist claims about scientific progress get detached from political claims about progress so as to found them, a detachment of which Foucault is deeply suspicious, becomes the main theme of the second half of their discussion as it turns to more straightforwardly political issues, remembering that this discussion took place in the aftermath of the events of 1968, the still burning flags of the civil rights movements and the protests against the Vietnam war (to name a few).

## Justice and Power

As the discussion turns to political themes the difference between Chomsky's version of the truth about politics and Foucault's version of the politics of truth becomes starkly articulated. Chomsky founds his opening summary of his political position by building directly on the naturalist and humanist claims that shaped his views on science, language and human nature: 'a fundamental element of human nature is the need for creative work, for creative inquiry, for free creation without the arbitrary effect of coercive institutions' (2006: 37). This provides the diagnostic basis for his critique of existing power structures, 'the elements of repression and oppression and destruction and coercion that exist in any existing society' based, for example on the institution of private property (2006: 38). Dismissing one of the tenets of liberal society, namely, that private property can be justified intrinsically, he calls for a period of transition in which 'meaningless drudgery' can be eliminated 'in favour of direct participation in the form of workers' councils' (2006: 38). Once such drudgery is eliminated, he claims, then a 'decentralized system of free associations' in all domains including the economic and political will enable 'the creative urge' that forms part of human nature to 'realize itself in whatever way it will' (2006: 38-39). In these opening remarks we can clearly discern the markers that accompany any claim based on the truth of politics: a grounding statement of human nature, a

diagnostic assessment of that which oppresses human nature, a theory of transition and a utopian vision that then brings the ground back to fruition, so to
speak. While Chomsky's version is what he refers to as 'anarcho-syndicalism',
these features are in fact present in all political ideologies that claim a direct
modern lineage (MacKenzie: 2014).

It is important to dwell on this for the moment. This same schema of
truth/diagnosis/transition/utopia shapes most of the political debate and
discussion that animates modern politics. This is true of the epochal debates that have shaped the modern world, such as those between commu-
nism and liberalism, but it is equally true of the national rivalries of left
and right that, even in our populist times, continue to shape the everyday
world of parliamentary democracies. Moreover, the subtle differences that
emerge within political ideologies can often be accounted for through the
different ways in which comradely disputes arise regarding one or other of
these main features: for example, the dispute about the politics of transition
that differentiated the suffragettes from the suffragists, or the divergences
regarding human nature and utopian hopes that splits the neo-liberal con-
servatives from those that give a high value to tradition. That Chomsky's
vision has an undeniably radical hue, and that it is a compelling vision of
free association and free creative endeavour, should not blind us to the fact
that the way in which his vision is articulated is fundamentally the same as
those of other, rival, political ideologies. It is this that Foucault has in mind
as he begins to articulate his politics of truth against Chomsky's claims
regarding the truth about politics.

There is clear agreement between Foucault and Chomsky that liberal
democracies are not as democratic as they claim to be. However, Foucault
admits that he is far less 'advanced' than Chomsky in his political views because he is not able to propose 'an ideal social model' (2006: 40). What this
really indicates, though, is not a claim about the advanced or not nature of
Foucault's views, rather it indicates the radically different approach he takes
to matters of political concern. It is a radically different approach because
his political views do not conform to the model of political ideologies that
dominates Western political discourse, seeing in the model itself some highly
questionable assumptions, as we have already seen, about the naturalism and
humanism animating these positions, including Chomsky's. His concerns
with this model are based on his historical perspective: he sceptically ponders
that the view of human nature grounding Chomsky's political vision might
be based on treating a historically specific and contingent feature of humanity, our sense of ourselves as free, creative agents, one linked to the emergence
of specific economic formations and particular understandings of the operation of power, as a universal feature of all humanity. In this sense, in fact,
Foucault raises against Chomsky a question that Rousseau raised against

Hobbes. Where Hobbes saw humanity as solipsistic to the point of fearful selfishness that bred competition for power that had the potential to create the conditions for 'a war of all against all' if it is left to run free without an absolute sovereign authority to hold that in check, Rousseau presented these allegedly universal features of humanity as a mere reflection of Hobbes' deep immersion within civil conflict and nascent forms of industrialisation and capitalism. But if that is the case then what is to prevent Foucault's version of the politics of truth simply becoming a different political ideology, structurally similar to Chomsky's, in the way that Rousseau's was structurally similar to Hobbes' social contract theory?

To borrow a phrase from Deleuze and Guattari (one to which we will return in Chapter 3), Foucault invites us to 'begin in the middle'. 'The real political task', he says, 'in a society such as ours is to criticise the workings of institutions, which appear to be both neutral and independent' (2006: 41). On the face of it, this is not so different from Chomsky's suggestion that we challenge the modern institutions that keep us in drudgery, but the addition of those institutions that 'appear neutral and independent' is what really marks the difference. For Foucault (2002a), even those social sciences that seem to offer radical challenges to the oppressive regimes of modernity are intimately bound up with forms of power that are much more subtle and less visible than is usually assumed. Crucially, these include the sciences of man from which we draw our vision of human nature; such as medicine and psychiatry (Foucault, 1965, 1973). If one fails to recognise the subtle support that these, and other, forms of knowledge provide for contemporary systems of domination and oppression then one risks grounding one's radical position on a view of human nature that surreptitiously upholds the very systems that one is trying to critique and resist. It is a lesson he takes to be been demonstrated by the communist revolutions of the twentieth century, revolutions in which class power was able to 'reconstitute itself even after an apparent revolutionary process' (Foucault, 2006: 41). Philosophically, the form of institutional critique Foucault envisages requires suspending all claims to human nature for fear that they are already too deeply implicated in the system one is trying to hold to account or overthrow. This similarly requires letting go of utopian visions founded on ideas of human nature; however one is to critique modern institutions it should not be motivated by the assumption of a possible world of free associations. We will delve more deeply into what Foucault has in mind by way of institutional critique in the next chapter, but we can glimpse what is at stake as we consider the differing accounts of justice and power that he and Chomsky offer in their discussion.

Both agree that the law, the legal system with all its regularities and practices, is one of the institutions of modern democracies that must be subject to critique and resisted when it can be shown to be working in the interests of some rather than all. Nonetheless, they differ quite profoundly on how one should conceive of challenges to legal systems. For Chomsky, one must differentiate those elements of the law that are 'an instrument of the powerful to retain their power' and those that enable and empower citizens to hold the state to account for its criminal actions, such as is the case with the American war in Vietnam or in the case of the Pentagon papers (the Watergate scandal) (2006: 48-49). Such differentiations can be made on the grounds of justice. But even here Chomsky is reflexive and subtle, saying that he is not interested in an ideal concept of justice but a 'better' one (2006: 50), thereby trying to ward off some of the normative assumptions that come with our defence of liberal democracies. The question remains, however, and it is one picked up by Foucault; how does one know a better from a worse conception of justice if one is not guided, in some sense, by an ideal conception? Foucault rightly refers to Chomsky as justifying his critique of legal systems 'in the name of a purer justice'. Chomsky's response is that of the practical activist. How could we engage in activism and resistance if we are not guided, as reasonable people, by a better conception of justice? And, in Foucault's response to this problem we get to the heart of their dispute about power and justice:

I would like to reply to you in terms of Spinoza and say that the proletariat doesn't wage war against the ruling class because it considers such a war to be just. The proletariat makes war with the ruling class because, for the first time on history, it wants to take power. And because it will overthrow the power of the ruling class, it considers such a war to be just. (2006: 51)

On the face of it, then, there is a simple reversal of Chomsky's terms. For Chomsky, justice does serve, at least in principle, as a regulative ideal to the extent that a 'better' justice can be known, and employed in ways that enable human beings to follow their nature as free, creative producers. For all the Marxist and anarcho-syndicalist tones of this view, it is guided by a Kantian notion of justice, where justice is that which, once properly articulated by rational beings, will order and regulate our activities in ways that prevent further oppressive systems of power; or, more positively, in ways that are in accordance with our nature. The Spinozist twist Foucault elaborates takes justice to be a practical device that is employed by those that seek to empower themselves. Whereas, for Chomsky, the unjust nature of legal systems can be established reasonably by reasonable persons in ways that then motivate, and legitimate, practices of resistance in the name of empowerment, for Foucault the question of power comes first and only then do questions of justice arise. According to Foucault, all of our relationships are relationships of power and it is not possible to regulate these out of existence through a correctly applied ideal of justice. Instead, it is important to see human empowerment within these complex relations of power as a feature motivating practices of resistance. That we sometimes, maybe even often, articulate our practice through the ideal of justice does not give any particular privilege to this idea, rather it is a strategic device for those seeking to empower themselves, and this often means 'taking power' from those that are thought to have it. Further hinting at a philosophical lineage that will become important as we develop the argument by turning this time not to a pre- but a post-Kantian, Foucault continues to question Chomsky's commitments to the importance of justice as an ideal to be employed against power, when he says:

I will be a little bit Nietzschean about this: it seems to me that the idea of justice in itself is an idea which in effect has been invented and put to work in different types of societies as an instrument of a certain political and economic power or as a weapon against that power. (2006: 54)

In this sense, and to elaborate the link between Spinoza and Nietzsche against Kant, justice is not a transcendent ideal that can be brought down to earth to justify practices of resistance, it is always already embedded within the very systems one is trying to resist in ways that mean it will only ever be so deeply embroiled in those systems that trying to mobilise against them in the name of justice will inevitably lead to forms of resistance becoming recuperated within the system itself. It is not that justice should not be used in struggles as a banner behind which to rally, it is precisely because it is implicated in the complex relations of power that shape any society that it will be used as such. However, for precisely this reason it will also be the case that it can never assume the form of an ideal against which to overthrow oppressive regimes, once and for all; so to speak. Should whole scale social transformation take place, as perhaps it did in the Communist regimes of the twentieth century, the question of justice does not disappear, rather it is reformulated according to the new relations of power that are embedded within these regimes. Chomsky's hope that one can differentiate between those regimes of justice that are really just and those that merely claim it, simply confirms the Kantian legacies of his normative social and political claims, even when shrouded in Marxist and anarchist terminology.

Drawing out an important element from the Introduction, we can see that what is at stake is a difference of opinion regarding *what happens* when we resist. Are we seeking to realize the truth of human nature against oppressive regimes in the name of justice? Or, are we seeking forms of empowerment within regimes that have disempowered us without deciding in advance if this will lead to a utopian future? We can pull this thread together with the others in this chapter by considering their respective views on revolution, perhaps the political event *par excellence*.

## Revolution and Transformation

As we look to understand practices of resistance it is commonplace to catego-
rise them, as either revolutionary or reformist. The former are typically those
that seek to enact sweeping social, economic and political changes, whereas
the latter are those that seek to amend current regimes in the name of making
them more inclusive, accountable, and responsive etc. while leaving the basic
structures intact. The question is one of ends: to what ends are practices of
resistance aimed? But what we are now in a position to understand is the question of ends is intimately, even necessarily, linked to the question of grounds,
or beginnings so to speak. If one assumes a version of human nature that is
being suppressed by the regime that one is protesting against then it is easy to
move seamlessly to the idea that one must change it with a view to enabling
our nature, however we define it, to flourish. This may require revolution or
reform, depending upon one's diagnosis of the oppressive regime and the po-
tentials or not it contains within it to realise human flourishing. Important
tactical and strategic questions follow for those who differ in their assessment
of the diagnosis. Fundamentally, though, both revolutionaries and reformists
share a structure of analysis that treats ends as conditioned by grounds, by a
view of human nature. We can see how this works in Chomsky's evocative radical humanism, which nonetheless equivocates on revolutionary and reformist
strategies. The question that follows is this: which is Foucault, revolutionary or
reformist? The answer, however, has already emerged in his views on science,
language and creativity; he is neither, instead his view can best be labelled a
politics of transformation 'in the middle' that eschews the dialectic of ends
and grounds. At stake is a substantially different conception of what happens
in practices of resistance, that we have glimpsed in his account of the complex
relation between justice and power even though it will not be fully elaborated
until the closing chapter of this book. In other words, just as Foucault refused
the traditional model of political ideologies, he also develops a different conception of the evental status of resistance that retains the critical inheritance
of his structuralist conception of schematism but in a manner that brings his
poststructuralist conception of change to the fore (for a developed Foucauldian
account of the event see, Foucault, 2002b).

Chomsky's cautious but committed radicalism has been noted several
times already. This same tone is adopted whenever he addresses the idea of
social and political change. He accepts, in response to Foucault, that it is important to subject the institutions of modern society that appear neutral to a
rigorous critique as this is often where 'autocratic control' resides. But where
Foucault sees this as necessarily requiring us to suspend the claims about human nature which have been shaped by these institutions, Chomsky thinks
that it would be a 'great shame to put aside entirely the somewhat more abstract

and philosophical task of trying to draw the connections between a concept of human nature that gives full scope to freedom and dignity and creativity and other fundamental human characteristics, and to relate that to some notion of social structure in which those properties could be realized and in which meaningful life takes place' (2006: 42). Armed with such a theory of human nature, it is then a matter of the local conditions as to whether or not we should engage in revolution or reform. Certain aspects of liberal democracies may allow for significant reforms that nonetheless enable the best features of democratic accountability to be taken forward. Other features seem to require that, at the least, violent struggle to overthrow the whole system should not be ruled out. How can we know the difference? Chomsky gives a simple answer, albeit one that does commit his radicalism to a certain privilege afforded the intellectual domain: 'one can and must give an argument' (2006: 56-57). There is, in other words, a keen rationalism linking his naturalism and humanism, where rationalism is the idea that human reason is equally shared among the species and that it can and should guide us to progressively better ways of living together in the world. He goes on:

Give an argument that the social revolution that you're trying to achieve *is* in the ends of justice, *is* in the ends of realizing fundamental human needs, not merely in the ends of putting some other group into power, because they want it. (2006: 57)

The argument will guide the ends, based on the grounds of human nature, and between the two the tactical matters of reform or revolution will be sorted out. In either case, however, those ends, grounds and arguments will always circumscribe the event of 'social revolution'. In a certain sense, what happens in practices of resistance, therefore, will always be secondary to what has already been decided through argument as the best way of realizing the ground in the end one is seeking. The event itself plays little role.

Foucault's immediate response to Chomsky's position is instructive, if initially oblique. He asks Elders if he has 'time to answer' and then 'how much' to which the response is 'two minutes'. Everybody laughs when he says, 'that is unjust' (2006: 57): to which Chomsky agrees, 'absolutely, yes'. What is crucial in these responses is that Foucault is already questioning the ways in which arguments are framed: the rules and regularities, in this case, of a televised discussion which sets limits on what can be said and what must therefore remain unsaid. It is telling because it immediately brings to the fore that all argument is set by such limits, that Foucault is (obliquely, for sure) calling into question Chomsky's belief in the rational power of argument to guide us to social revolution by exposing the structures that exist which delimit argument itself. This is confirmed when he states that there is no argument between him and Chomsky on the theory of human nature, they simply 'understand each other very well' (2006: 57). At which point, it is clear that Foucault does not hold Chomsky's rationalist belief in the power of argument to sway us one way or another in purely theoretical disputes. Instead, it is clear from all of the conversation that he wishes simply to demarcate the dispute at the theoretical level as exactly that, and in some sense beyond the scope of rational resolution. Were he to leave it at that, though, this might seem to lead to a defeatist form of scepticism. However, he follows it up with the claim that where the real difference is to be found between them is when 'we discussed the problem of human nature and political problems' (2006: 57). Foucault is drawing Chomsky 'into the middle', to recall the phrase used above, so as to dispute the value of thinking first about grounds and then implying seamlessly a set of ends to be realized, whether through reform or revolution. Only when human nature is treated as intrinsic to the economic, social and political formations in which it emerged as an idea can it be seen what is really at stake. But if one does this then one cannot separate out the theory from the practice, give priority to the former over the latter, and then impute a set of tactics and strategies from the theory. Instead, for Foucault, one must intervene 'in the middle', in the domain of institutions that have 'superimposed' the idea of subject and progress on to the whole order of the production of knowledge in ways that mean it is not possible to separate knowledge from power. It is not possible, therefore, to separate the truths that our knowledge of the world can produce from the production of relations of power that condition those forms of the knowledge in the first place.

Questions of reform or revolution must, therefore, be suspended because this dialectic relies upon the whole framework of grounds and ends that cannot be justified in the abstract, as Chomsky hopes. In another perhaps oblique moment in the discussion, that in fact turned out to be Foucault's last intervention, Foucault refers to the diagnostic element of traditional humanist practices of resistance and calls into the question the idea that one must know the disease in order to cure the symptoms. He says instead that modern society is afflicted in a particular sort of way, 'the symptom itself brought the disease into being' (2006: 59). The importance of this, aside from the connection it makes to Foucault's (1965) famous discussions of madness, is that we can see just how unusual his politics of truth really is, in that the usual causal sequence is called into question. The upshot is a view of resistance that starts with the symptom and seeks to transform it, without presuming that there is an underlying, prior disease that must be known first and then treated discretely.

This implies a different view of the events that have transformed society in the past and therefore of those that may transform it in the present and future. Something happened within society that made us diagnose a prior cause, but in order to address this we must transform that which happened and in doing so we will then, no doubt, produce a different diagnosis of what was and is at stake for our future (see also Foucault 2002b). This is not such a difficult idea and it is interesting to note that Foucault makes this allusion in the context of a brief comment about psychiatry. For the psychiatrist, it is evident that we can feel a certain way because we have a sense of what happened to us in the past while if we change the way that we feel then we change what we think is crucial about our past, as well as opening up new potential ways of being in the future. The traumatic event is only traumatic because we think it was brought about by the event; but if we change how we feel about the event then it loses its diagnostic quality and other events typically come to have a deeper significance for us. This does not make them true, it merely means that we are able to change our sense of ourselves, our sense of the past, in the present at the symptomatic level, in ways that enable us to transform what we think is possible. Foucault presents this model, in a certain sense, as that which can shake us out of the traditional models of political ideologies based as they are on competing accounts of the truth about politics, and in doing so provides a politics of truth that is sceptical of those accounts but nonetheless non-defeatist. Events can be transformative and so we should look to transform ourselves, including our social, economic and political regimes, by reconfiguring the events that have shaped us. This is neither revolutionary nor reformist, but a transformative politics of the truth. We will see the detail of what this looks like from the perspective of Foucault's institutional critique, his account of the ethical relationship between the subject and truth and how this relates to the problem of how theory relates to practice in the next chapter.

# Chapter 2: Truth and Power

In the previous chapter we excavated the assumptions lying beneath two very different models of political theory. The model adopted by Chomsky relies upon naturalist and universalist claims about human nature that guide further claims about the truth of our political situation in ways which, it is hoped, will engender our resistance to, maybe revolution against, any institutions that stem human flourishing. In contrast, we saw how Foucault calls into question the naturalism, humanism and universalism of Chomsky's position by interrogating the historical and political status of truth, especially with a view to exposing the contingency embedded within claims regarding the truth of our nature as humans. This chapter will reconstruct Foucault's approach to the politics of truth in more detail and in a more positive spirit, on its own terms.

The focus will be on 'mid' and 'late' Foucault beginning with the discussion 'Truth and Power' (1980 [1977]) but moving on toward the equally seminal 'Subjectivity and Truth' (1997 [1980]). The former text is particularly useful because it brings together a number of important Foucauldian themes and concepts in a concise manner: that modern day institutions are the mediators of power and knowledge; that the politics of truth requires a genealogy of these institutions; that the notions of discourse and disciplinary society connect to an analytic of power that establishes its networked and productive character; that all claims to the truth by and about humans have an institutional expression that both fixes their status but that also enables their critique. How exactly this critique is to become expressed in modes of resistance, though, remained a vexed question in Foucault's work. Developing the ideas of the latter text, however, it will be argued that the idea of 'technique' is precisely the juncture at which power and knowledge operate institutionally but also, therefore the juncture at which the subject can direct critical attention and engage in practices of resistance. The closing section will then address the relationship between Foucault's avowed critique of the subject with this apparent return to the subject but it will do so through a broader discussion of theory and practice. All the while, the argument is centred on the problem of what is required of resistance when truth and power are as intimately and institutionally linked as Foucault claims.

## The Role of Institutions

We noted in the previous chapter that one of the key points of similarity and difference between Chomsky and Foucault relates to their respective interpretations of Kant's idea of the schema that unites intuition and understanding into knowledge. Chomsky adopts the standard humanist view that such schemas are located in the human mind and universally shared. Foucault adopts the structuralist revision of this idea and places the schema outside the human mind, in the social and political world. This means that, for Foucault, knowledge is possible only through a series of institutions that shape and guide such knowledge. However, we also noted that Foucault adopts the poststructuralist idea that such structures and the institutions through which they function are not universal features of human social existence but historically contingent and changeable. In 'Truth and Power' he gives a succinct account of why he has a problem with the structuralist position: an overemphasis on 'analyses couched in terms of the symbolic field or the domain of signifying structures' tends towards underemphasising the role of 'relations of force, strategic developments, and tactics' (1980: 147). Where the structuralists tended to interpret all phenomena (whether social, cultural, psychological, economic, political and so on) in terms of language and signs, Foucault prefers analyses that stress the role of 'war and battle' such that 'the history that bears and determines us has the form of a war rather than that of a language – relations of power, not relations of meaning' (1980: 147). When imbued with struggle and relations of power, structuralism can avoid surreptitiously affirming the 'calm Platonic form of language and dialogue' (1980: 147). Such a 'calm Platonism' tends to erase the precise detail of historical struggles in its search for linguistic universals and communicative rules that generate meaning. Being attentive to these struggles will necessitate analyses that presume the complex weave of meaning with power. In this way, the analyst can avoid treating the symbolic domain as if it were analogous to the abstracted forms of Plato's idealist philosophy. He is acutely aware, however, that even such a strongly historicist account can reinstate the priority of meaning he seeks to avoid if history itself is understood as a progressive series of ever more coherent claims that bring us closer to the truth, even through 'war and battles'. The most important versions of this claim are all forms of the dialectical philosophy outlined by Hegel. It is as important to distance his politics of truth from such positions, as it is to distance it from structuralism (for all that he remains a structuralist in many important respects). At stake is the question of whether or not history as a whole has meaning and Foucault is clear: 'history has no "meaning", though this is not to say that it is absurd or incoherent' (1980: 147). While he remains committed to the idea that historical material can be discussed and analysed in the minutest detail, the intelligibility of this detail must be framed 'in accordance with the intelligibility of struggles' (1980: 147). Situating such struggles within the overarching framework of the meaningfulness of historical advancement, as in dialectics, is 'a way of evading the always open and hazardous reality of conflict by reducing it to a Hegelian skeleton' (1980: 147). Even when the history of struggle is brought into our analyses of the construction of meaning it can still revert to abstraction if it is presumed that these struggles are imbued with an overarching logic, the dialectic, that shapes and frames their richly textured nature but that in doing so loses their multiplicitous and combative emergence. If we assume that struggles over meaningfulness always point toward an over-arching struggle for recognition and the pursuit of absolute knowledge (Hegel, 1977) then we lose the ability to analyse those struggles from within their historical milieu and we lose the ability to assess what such struggles might really mean for us, today. Therefore, the institutions that bear the struggles that mark the politics of truth should be carefully analysed in ways that avoid calm Platonism and skeletal Hegelianism. But what kind of analysis can achieve this dual goal?

Foucault's answer is genealogy. One of the problems with structuralism and dialectics is that they treat structure and history as akin to the subject of humanism; that is, as meaning generating conditions of all knowledge. If we are to dispense with humanism in all its forms then one has 'to dispense with the constituent subject, to get rid of the subject itself, that's to say, to arrive at an analysis that can account for the constitution of the subject within a historical framework' (1980: 150). Even, and perhaps especially, where this subject is hidden in the idea of structure or history. It is this form of historical analysis that does not presume a constituent subject that Foucault calls genealogy;

that is, a form of history that can account for the constitution of knowledges, discourses, domains of objects and so on, without having to make reference to a subject that is either transcendental in relation to the field of events or runs in its empty sameness throughout the course of history'. (1980: 150)

Two questions immediately present themselves: what are the objects of such genealogical analyses such that a calm Platonism is avoided? And, how are historical events to be understood such that a skeletal Hegelianism can be avoided?

The first of these questions leads us to some of the most directly influential notions of Foucault's entire oeuvre; the notions of discourse and the 'disciplinary grid' of society within which such discourses function. We saw already in the previous chapter that Foucault does not accept the idea of a progressive methodical maturation of medical knowledge in the eighteenth century, and 'the great man' thesis that lies behind such a view. Foucault prefers instead to focus on the ways in which the transformation of medical knowledge was superimposed upon and within other domains such as economics and politics. In this sense, it is not possible to disarticulate the claims of biology from those that were also animating these other domains. The object of Foucault's gene-alogical analyses, therefore, are the 'discursive regimes' operating within and between such disciplines. But what is a discourse? Foucault gives a particularly succinct answer in 'Truth and Power', referring once again to the emergence of modern medicine: 'the ways of speaking and seeing, the whole ensemble of practices which served as supports for medical knowledge' (1980: 144). It is important to dwell on this formulation. Immediately we notice that discourse is not just speaking, it is not just a way of ordering what is said. Rather, discourse orders ways of seeing and forms of practice and these are given every bit as much importance as what is said. Furthermore, it is clear that Foucault is not simply defining any particular discourse in terms of its content (that which is said, seen and practiced) but that the discourse refers to 'the ways of speaking and seeing' and the ways in which practices support knowledge. In this sense, Foucault is not inviting us to focus on the content of medical knowledge, for example, but on the ways in which what counts as medical knowledge is for-mulated and engendered. As he says, the task of foregrounding discourse is to understand 'the rules of formation of statements which are accepted as scien-tifically true' (1980: 144), rather than simply the statements themselves. What is crucial is that these rules are not to be confused with the methodologies of the natural and social sciences because they operate on a different level. They operate before such methodological questions emerge because what counts as legitimate in terms of what can be said, seen and practiced is what conditions those methodologies in the first place. However, we also know that for Fou-cault the historian, these rules change and his genealogical investigations into eighteenth century medicine and imprisonment, for example, are detailed in-vestigations into the small yet momentous 'modifications' that preside over the formulation of statements in these respective domains; modifications at the level of what counts in terms of what can be said, seen and practiced. As he puts it, these rules for the formation of scientific statements *govern* what counts as true: politics comes before method in the constitution of knowledge. In this sense, genealogy avoids the calm Platonism of a focus on language and mean-ing that he diagnoses in structuralism and is, instead, an investigation into 'what effects of power circulate among scientific statements, what constitutes, as it were, their internal regime of power, and how and why at certain moments that regime undergoes a global modification' (1980: 145).

But how can we square this idea of the rules that govern the formation of statements within particular domains and disciplines with the idea that these disciplines are always superimposed upon each other in complicated ways such that modifications in one area can lead to modifications in another?

Foucault's answer is that we must understand the 'grid' that operates across these domains, that governs them, as an object of analysis in its own right. At this point in the development of his ideas, the problem that fascinated him was that of the *disciplinary* grid of modern society. Famously developed in *Discipline and Punish*, Foucault (1980 [1977]) provides a compelling account of how the very idea of the disciplines, playing on the ambiguity of rules that govern us and rules for the formation of knowledge, emerged alongside the idea of the liberties so characteristic of modern liberal societies. Whereas the liberal narrative of its own revolutionary emergence stresses the freedoms acquired through successive challenges to feudal and sovereign power, Foucault patiently reconstructs the accompanying disciplinary techniques that enabled the government of these newly free subjects (1980: 223). Of paramount importance in this development were the institutions of the human sciences as it was these that sought to formulate what is required of the 'normal individual' in terms of their economic, social and political behaviour as well as their health and well-being. The normative claims of liberal political theory, therefore, are indistinguishable from the institutional processes of normalisation that govern what it means to be a free individual. In this way, by the time of his genealogical investigations, Foucault has situated his analyses of the discursive regimes which govern the production of truth within a broader analysis of the political struggles embedded within the emergence of liberal societies. Fundamentally, this is a struggle between empowering people to claim their freedom while also disciplining them to be normal individuals through the complex array of powerful institutions that characterise liberal democracies. As this formulation suggests, there is a complex understanding of power at work in Foucault's politics of truth.

As recognised by Foucault, his analyses of the emergence of modern medicine and other disciplines during his archaeological investigations of the 1960's, tended to assume the problem of power but not tackle it directly (1980: 145). The danger with such an assumption is that the idea of power itself can smuggle back into the analyses aspects of the humanism that he has tried so hard to avoid, by virtue of treating power as something that is held by one subject against, or over and above, another. This is indeed the way that power is usually conceptualised by both the right and left of modern liberal democracies: either power is embodied in the sovereign as expressed in social contract theory, or it is embedded in the class dynamics of industrial societies as expressed in Marxism and socialism. What neither of these positions allows, according to Foucault, is a thorough and detailed analysis of the 'mechanisms of power' that both enable liberty and the disciplines. For that to be the case, we must move beyond the idea of power as repressive and consider the 'fact', that it doesn't only weigh on us as a force that says no; it also traverses and produces things, it induces pleasure, forms knowledge and produces discourse. It needs to be considered as a productive network that runs through the whole social body, much more than as a negative instance whose function is repression. (1980: 153) etc.

This quote, the analysis of *Discipline and Punish* from which it draws and the crisp analytic of power summarised in *The History of Sexuality: An Introduction* (1978 [1976]), have all been very widely discussed and this is not the place to rehearse these debates (for an excellent discussion of Foucault's analytic of power see, Widder: 2004). What is important is Foucault's tireless effort to root out all vestiges of humanism from within his politics of truth. Recognising the 'internal regime of power' that shapes the rules that govern the formulation of statements is not enough, if it does not also come with a new theorisation of power that challenges the typical view that it is a substance that can be used by one political actor against another. Understanding power as a relational phenomenon that constitutes all identities, all political actors, enables the investigation of 'a whole series of multiple and indefinite power relations that supply the necessary basis for the great negative forms of power' (1980: 157). That said, these same 'multiple and indefinite power relations' provide the necessary basis for the inducement of pleasure, the formation of knowledge and the production of discourse. Only once such complexities are grasped, according to Foucault, will we be able to 'cut off the king's head' in political theory, because it is only then that we will be able to see the way power functions both productively and prohibitively; even if prohibitions are the result of power relations and even if they are the forms of power that are most acutely experienced, they are still conditioned by the multiple and complex networks of power that must have analytical priority.

For all that Foucault's unflinching critique of humanism digs deeply into the battlefield of discursive regimes to avoid the calm Platonism of a certain type of structuralism, there is something cosily reassuring about the picture that appears to be emerging. It seems that he is veering dangerously close to the construction of an overarching narrative of disciplinary society that gives meaning to the particular operation of power within modern institutions that shape the alleged truths of our human nature. Is there not a risk of reintroducing the skeletal Hegelianism that he sought to avoid? For all his wariness with regard to progress, is there the danger that his genealogical investigations will render meaningful a better account of how power and truth are interlinked in ways that must assume some notion of progress through knowledge? What is the status of his genealogical investigations vis-à-vis the truth, in general? These questions will guide the next section of this chapter. However, we can get an important hint of what is involved in retaining Foucault's genealogical intentions against such slippage if we remind ourselves of the second question that shaped this section; how are historical events to be understood such that a skeletal Hegelianism can be avoided?

Foucault is clear about the risks: 'it is not a matter of locating everything on one level, that of the event' (1980: 146-7) as this would tend toward an analysis of the emergence of the disciplinary grid of society and the discourses it orders in terms of the 'negativity' he found so troubling at the heart of Chomsky's account of the progress of the sciences, natural and human. Rather, he says, the task is to realize 'that there are actually a whole order of levels of different types of events differing in amplitude, chronological breadth, and capacity to produce effects' (1980: 147). In other words, one must avoid ordering the chaos of the battlefield of power relations by placing it under the umbrella of the great battle that changed everything. There is no point replacing the 'great man' thesis with the 'great battle' thesis, for all the same problems will re-emerge. What must be challenged is the greatness of whatever happened such that it's mundane and banal nature can be properly understood; genealogy, as Foucault says in a different context, is 'grey, meticulous and patiently documentary' (1992: 139). It is this careful approach to the detail of what happened, that allows the genealogist 'to distinguish among events, to differentiate the networks and levels to which they belong, and to reconstitute the lines along which they are connected and engender one another' (1980: 147). It is precisely this eye for detailed differentiation of historical events, and the connections between them, that puts flesh on the bones of discursive modifications within the disciplinary grid of modern society that leaves the skeletal Hegelianism looking as bare as it is really is, in terms of explaining anything about how we have got to be where we are now. Instead of a great battle that inaugurated liberal societies and their disciplinary institutions, therefore, it is important to be alive to the multiple local modifications that have resonated or not with each other in ways that have shaped the complex institutional world in which we live, in modern liberal societies.

In an echo of the conversation with Chomsky, Foucault takes this idea forward into how he thinks about what is meant by revolution: 'there are many different kinds of revolution, roughly speaking, as many kinds as there are possible subversive recodifications of power relations' (1980: 157). Because the oppressive state was not constituted through one big battle that saw capitalism victorious, the workers will not overthrow it in one even more historically seismic revolution. Rather, there are multiple sites of revolutionary activity, even if some of these will leave the power embedded within the state 'essentially untouched'. One again we see that giving up on origins and grounds means giving up on a single end; but in place of these we get multiple grounds, multiple events operating at many different levels, that each contain the possibility for resisting their effects. We will see why this is the case in the next chapter. For now, it is important to specify whether or not even this genealogical account of institutions, networks of power and multiple events is enough to ward off the problem of the persistent return of truth, without the politics.

## Ideology and Truth

What we might call the problem of ideology is a particularly pointed version of the problem identified above as the surreptitious reintroduction of a skeletal Hegelianism. Certainly, this is the case if ideology is understood in a broadly Marxist sense, as it was for Foucault, and to the extent that Marx is a direct disciple and heir to Hegel as much as his most vehement critic. In general terms, the problem is this: if one makes a claim that presents the underlying logic of contemporary society then what is to stop the counter-claim emerging that one's own claim already reflects that underlying logic, in ways that paralyse the analysis? Amongst students of ideology this is a well-known paradox (MacKenzie: 2016). Critics of ideology, who present the truth about the mechanisms that shape our ideas in order to diagnose the ideological components of contemporary debates, risks the counter-claim that they are in fact merely ideologues of the very system that they seek to criticise. Logically, it becomes a version of the liar's paradox: how can we know that the person supposedly telling the truth about everyone else's lies, is not also lying? For Foucault, there is a more immediate set of concerns, however. It is clear in 'Truth and Politics' and elsewhere, that Foucault was deeply influenced by what he felt was the overbearing effect of Marxism within the French academy (he describes his early investigations as 'timid and hesitant' (1980: 143) as a result) while equally being liberated from this sense to study power by the events of 1968 and the failures, as he sees it, of Marxists to anticipate or understand these events. Nonetheless, it is a concept and a problem that he must address and in this text he gives his most famous and succinct account of why he thinks the notion of ideology is 'difficult to make use of' (1980: 152). He gives three reasons, and it worth spending time reconstructing these as they go a long way toward clarifying aspects of his politics of truth and, as we will see, how such a politics may still motivate practices of resistance.

Foucault's first objection to the idea of ideology is that 'like it or not, it always stands in virtual opposition to something else that is supposed to count as truth' (1980: 152). Given the Marxist conception of ideology that he has in mind, there is nothing too controversial in this claim, as most, if not all, Marxists would maintain that this is precisely the point of the concept. The ideas that dominate contemporary liberal and capitalist societies are false ideas, precisely because they represent the interests of the bourgeois class, and exposing the truth of this claim a dialectical and materialist account of history animates resistance to them. We saw a version of this in Chomsky's position, in the previous chapter. It is also clear why Foucault objects to this position. His politics of truth focuses on the political conditions that generate the meaningfulness of truth claims in ways that undermine the progressivist assumptions of any dialectical position, including Marxism. In this text, though, he clarifies an important part of this project: 'I believe that the problem does not consist in drawing a line between that which, in a discourse, falls under the category of scientificity or truth, and that which comes under some other category; rather, it consists in seeing historically how effects of truth are produced within discourses that, in themselves, are neither true nor false' (1980: 152). It is this last clarification that is striking: the analyses he offers of the ways of speaking, seeing and practicing that legitimate what counts as true or false are not in themselves true or false. This is clearly a necessary conclusion if he is to avoid the paradoxes of ideology critique but it is not immediately evident what this could mean. What is the status of his investigations if they are neither true nor false? In fact, Foucault does not elaborate on this claim at this point and it is left hanging rather provocatively in the air. We shall see in a moment one of the ways in which he articulates a response to this issue as he turns to the role of the intellectual in contemporary societies. We will, however, have to delve more deeply as the argument of this book develops by turning to his later work on subjectivity and truth but also, in the next chapter, to the philosophy of difference presented by Deleuze in *Difference and Repetition*. For now, we can glimpse some of the issues as we follow Foucault's 'circumspection' about the idea of ideology.

Foucault's second and third reasons for distrusting the idea of ideology is familiar from his discussion with Chomsky. Foucault rightly points out that 'the concept of ideology refers, I think necessarily, to something of the order of a subject' (1980: 152). We have already discussed his reticence about any analyses that contain such subjective presuppositions. It is important to note, nonetheless, that his caveat 'I think necessarily' is interesting because it establishes his position vis-à-vis the allegedly structuralist rendering of ideology developed by Althusser (2008). Even such a structuralist account, we can infer, will not escape the 'order of the subject' because it presumes that there is a subject, the proletariat for example, that is able to know the conditions of its own constitution in ways that will enable their revolutionary transformation. Moreover, and this relates to Foucault's third concern with the notion of ideology, it seems impossible to import the idea of ideology into one's analyses without presuming that 'ideology stands in a secondary position relative to something that functions as its infrastructure, as its material, economic determinant' (1980: 152). That ideas are presented as having this secondary status, for Foucault, can only be maintained if it is thought that critics of ideology are able to transcend their entrenchment in ideology and assume that their analyses have direct access to the primary, in this case economic, mechanisms that determine our ideas.

Not only is such an assumption poorly founded philosophically, it is dangerous politically; dangerous because it creates the atmosphere that has those who think differently denounced as purveyors of false ideas and, in extremis, punished and killed for those beliefs. In general, though, assuming that there is a subject that can know the truth of its situation while others do not inevitably tends toward claims that set up grounds and shape ends in ways that Foucault, the genealogist of complex overlapping events and discourses, can not accept because it reduces the intricate weave of struggles, powers and relations to simple narratives unable to sustain their own truth claims in anything other than a viciously circular manner. But what of Foucault's own investigations and their status if they are neither true nor false?

In 'Truth and Power' Foucault is asked this directly: 'if one isn't an "organic" intellectual acting as the spokesman for a global organisation, if one doesn't purport to function as the bringer, the master of truth, what position is the intellectual to assume?' (1980: 161). Foucault's response was written after the interview was conducted and it contains a famous and fascinating account of how he saw his role, if it was not to be a 'master of truth'. Foucault contextualises his answer to the question in a historical account of the changing role of the intellectual in the modern period: where once intellectuals were deemed to operate in the 'universal' mode, as 'the man of justice' for all, they have, since the end of the second world war, become increasingly focused on specific sectors such as housing, the hospital, the economy, and so on. In this respect, Foucault is closely aligned with the analysis of specialisation that emerged from the Frankfurt School. But where second generation Frankfurt School analysis retained its optimism of universalism, Foucault takes a different route. For all that he is critical of specialisation in the ways that it plays into the hands of disciplinary institutions, he sees in this new specificity a chance for a different kind of intellectual response to the times, one that does not imply the need for a universal account of justice. This response is contained in the idea of the specific intellectual.

The specific intellectual, according to Foucault, may well be an expert trapped to some extent within the modern apparatuses of the disciplinary institutions of the state but it is also a figure that is able to connect more deeply to the actual material concerns of the 'proletariat or the masses' because of this expertise. Even more importantly, this expertise with regard to the material conditions of real people enables 'a global process of politicisation', albeit one bereft of the desire for justice that shaped the universal intellectual of the early modern period. This global process takes a different form and, in a particularly striking and prescient image, Foucault characterises it as one of 'exchange'. The specific intellectual, comfortable in their own particular domains of expertise, is nonetheless also aware of the limits of their disciplinary discursive regimes to the point where they can see how these may connect at 'privileged points of intersection' (1980: 163). We can detect here an echo of Foucault's concern with the multiplicity of discourses, the overlapping events of different chronologies and amplitude that have shaped them, his insistence that we avoid not just the great man but also the great battle thesis. His complex genealogies of the emergence of discursive regimes gives him a ready-made eye for the detail of how complex the relations between them are, but also a way of articulating what may be done in order to resist their disciplinary effects. Rather than transcend this diversity, resistance is to be found by the intellectual process of exchanging ideas between disciplines, ideas that are shaped under one discursive domain but can cause rupture and change within another. It is precisely because modern experts are employed in the service of disciplinary institutions that they can exchange ideas between them in the service of resisting these same institutions: 'one may even say that the role of the specific intellectual must become more and more important in proportion to the political responsibilities which he is obliged to accept' (1980: 167). This is the case because 'local, specific struggle can have effects and implications that are not simply professional or sectoral' (1980: 169) where this is understood as a struggle with regard to the ways in which saying, seeing and practicing legitimate discursive regimes. He says, 'it's not a matter of a battle "on behalf" of truth but of a battle about the status of truth and the economic and political role it plays' (1980: 170). Exchanging these battles across disciplinary and discursive formations involves redrawing the networks of power operating within society, 'not in terms of "science" and "ideology" but in terms of "truth" and "power". And thus the question of the professionalization of intellectuals and manual labour can be envisaged in a new way' (1980: 170).

There is something compelling and invigorating about Foucault's vision of how the specific intellectual may resist the dangerous effects of the intellectual specialisation associated with modernisation. In contemporary parlance, it is the potential of rigorous interdisciplinary work or, better yet, transdisciplinary work in which the most fundamental aspects of our disciplines are exchanged across fields of inquiry in ways that shake the foundations of who we think we are as human beings, including our place in nature. Current transdisciplinary concerns with the anthropocene are a case in point (se, for example, Moore: 2016). However, there are justifiable concerns with Foucault's vision lurking not too far from the surface. Is it a privilege of intellectuals to be able to resist disciplinary norms? If so, then what of the mass of people who have no such privileged access to the fundamentals of the natural and human sciences? Is it also a concern that this image of the intellectual seems to valorise a certain form of individualism that may have the 'great man', now as the 'great exchanger of ideas', return despite Foucault's avowed distrust of such an idea? What of the power of collectives, groups and masses to shake and unsettle modern disciplinary institutions? These concerns will be addressed in the remaining sections of this chapter, but is important first to dwell a little longer on what it is that specific intellectuals produce through such acts of resistance through exchange.

Foucault ends his written response with six tentative 'propositions' that sum up his politics of truth. The first three neatly encapsulate the themes developed so far in this discussion: 1) '"truth" is to be understood as a system of ordered procedures for the production, regulation, distribution, circulation and operation of statements. 2) "Truth" is linked in a circular relation with systems of power that produce and sustain it, and to effects of power which it induces and which extend it – a "regime" of truth. 3) This regime is not merely ideological or superstructural; it was a condition of the formation and development of capitalism' (1980: 170). Furthermore, the last proposition neatly summarises his project in ways that refer us back to the paradoxes of ideology critique with which we began this section: 'The political question, to sum up, is not error, illusion, alienated consciousness, or ideology; it is truth itself' (1980: 171). However, in the fourth and fifth propositions we get two intriguing formulations that give us a better understanding of what exactly is at stake in his response to this political question; or, in other words, what is at stake for the specific intellectual in resisting their professionalization by embracing it and exchanging with others in different domains. It is worth quoting these propositions in full:

The essential political problem for the intellectual is not to criticise the ideological contents supposedly linked to science, or to ensure that his own scientific practice is accompanied by a correct ideology, but that of ascertaining the possibility of constituting a new politics of truth. The problem is not changing people's consciousness - or what's in their heads - but the political, economic, institutional regime of the production of truth.

It's not a matter of emancipating truth from every system of power (which would be a chimera, for truth is already power) but of detaching the power of truth from the forms of hegemony, social, economic, and cultural, within which it operates at he present time (1980: 171-2).

While it is tempting to read these as simple restatements of the first three propositions in preparation for the last, they do in fact add two significant claims that need to be highlighted. First, it is clear that Foucault does not envisage the specific intellectual as one that can emancipate us from the regimes of truth but as a figure that can engage in the constitution of 'a new politics of truth'. The task of the 'exchanger', therefore, is not simply to expose the political struggles behind the calm surface of truth but to propose new truths that will, inevitably, circulate around and within new networks of power. The politics of truth as a practice of resistance is not defined by simply dismantling the idea of the truth but by creating truths that will unsettle the disciplinary and discursive regimes within which we are defined as 'normal' human beings. The criteria for the establishment of such 'new truths' is given in the fifth proposition: they will retain 'the power of truth' but in ways that are detached from hegemonic institutions. That Foucault still aligns truth with this power is an important feature of his overall project of a politics of truth. But does it not risk, once again, a surreptitious recuperation of the humanist, naturalist and universalist model that he is so determined to disavow?

This would be the case if we were to focus on the 'new politics of truth' as the production of new statements. But it is clear that Foucault envisages this task as one in which the conditions for such true statements are changed, conditions which in themselves as we saw above, are neither true nor false. We have had a hint of what this means in the many small revolutions envisaged by Foucault, based on his intricate account of the different events that have shaped modern disciplinary societies. It is now possible to say that what he has in mind with such a politics of truth is a politics that operates at the level of these events in order to reinscribe their effects as bearers of truth in new ways. But how does one change events? This question will come into focus in the next chapter. For now, we must deal with the lingering concerns that Foucault's idea of a 'new politics of truth' places too much emphasis on individuals, in particular the individual intellectual as bearer of a new politics of truth.

### Who are we to criticise?

There is a common misunderstanding about Foucault's later work on the self. It is often thought that he renounced his earlier poststructuralist analyses because he had to acknowledge that they relied too heavily on the idea of the 'docile self' (*Discipline and Punish*); a view of the self that was unsustainable not least because it robbed individuals of the power to change the world around them (for example, McNay: 1994). As we have seen above, the problem faced by Foucault is rather different. He was aware throughout his scholarly work of the ever-present problem of the return of the constituent self, in all it's guises; in the surreptitious humanism of the structure, the overarching humanism of treating history itself as the subject that determines meaningfulness, the difficulties of progressive views of science and politics that tend to imply a great man view of history and even the dangers in his own genealogies of struggles becoming read as a version of a great battle thesis that would simply replay these problems on another level, within a different framework. Moreover, his appeal to the role that can be played by specific intellectuals in the exchange of discursive practices as a form of resistance to disciplinary mechanisms also creates the impression that resistance to the social formations and institutions that characterise the modern world may itself lead to a return to a kind of individualism indebted to the humanism he sought so vigorously to avoid. So, rather than see his later work on the self as a turn away from his archaeological investigations into the discursive regimes of knowledge creation, or a turn away from the genealogical investigations into the power relations embedded within these regimes of knowledge in order to recover human agency and the self, we should see his later work as an attempt to root out the last vestiges of humanism from within these earlier works by considering the intricate and subtle ways in which the constituted (rather than constituent) self is implicated in regimes of knowledge and power in complex economic, social and political formations that shape what we take to be the truth about ourselves. The late work, therefore, is not a valorisation of the self against his poststructuralist critique of the subject; it is an attempt to give a more thorough a-humanist account of how the self is constructed from within longstanding regimes that make it difficult to escape the idea that if we know ourselves then we will know the truth that will free us from domination. 'Subjectivity and Truth' is an excellent example of how Foucault tackles these themes and as such it provides a compelling framework for analyses regarding who we are, as modern subjects, and who we are to criticise the regimes that shape our sense of self in the modern disciplinary world.

For Foucault, in order to root out the last vestiges of humanism we must look more thoroughly at the 'strange and complex relationships developed in our societies between individuality, discourse, truth and coercion' (1997: 148). His overarching goal is a genealogy of the modern subject, an analysis of the ways in which we have come to think of ourselves as subjects that have a particular relationship to truth. As in earlier work, he situates this against those forms of philosophy that have retained a sense of the constituent subject at their core; in this context he talks of Descartes, Husserl, Sartre and forms of humanist Marxism. Although he acknowledges that modern philosophy has developed sophisticated alternatives to these forms of subject-centred philosophy in positivism and structuralism he proposes genealogy as an alternative because, as we know, he views both of these alternatives as ones that simply reinstate the privilege of the subject as that which knows the truth. But what does Foucault add to his earlier analyses?

We can think of this in two ways. On the one hand, he brings into view the ways in which the subject enacts its own constituted nature, while, on the other hand, he takes a longer historical sweep for his genealogy of the subject because he sees these forms of enactment as more deeply rooted in Western culture than in the modern period he has analysed previously. The former brings into view a concern with *techne*, whereas the latter provides insight into the idea that modern philosophies of the subject are still embroiled within the 'Delphic precept' to 'know yourself'. His guiding assumption is that if we can understand the techniques that have been employed by the self in order to know itself then we can understand both how these shape modern conceptions of the subject and how they may be challenged and critiqued. What we will see is that Foucault's analyses provide an account of the techniques of the self that can be mobilised in practices of resistance, if we always remember that these techniques of the self are simply examples of the revolutionary gestures that can operate on the multiple layers of the events that have shaped our sense of who we are, even if they are events that reach back into the foundations of the Western idea of the subject.

Foucault develops the idea of technique in three ways. First, he situates his interest in technology within post-WWII critiques of technology from the Frankfurt School. Referring to Habermas's discussion in *Knowledge and Human Interests*, Foucault says, 'it seems one can identify three major types of techniques in human societies...techniques of production, techniques of signification, and techniques of domination' (1997: 153). Candidly suggesting that he has not been concerned with the first two he does say that 'since my project was concerned with the knowledge of the subject, I thought that the techniques of domination were the most important' (1997: 153). But he also immediately adds to this that as his interests shifted to 'the experience of sexuality' he became 'more and more aware' that there is another type of technique that must be addressed. He summarises what he has in mind:

techniques which permit individuals to perform, by their own means, a certain number of operations on their own bodies, on their own souls, on their own thoughts, on their own conduct, and this in such a way that they transform themselves, modify themselves, and reach a certain state of perfection, of happiness, of purity, of supernatural power, and so on (1997: 154).

He calls these techniques or technologies of the self. The crucial point, as he acknowledges, is that these techniques of the self are in a complicated relation to techniques of domination. If we are to understand the ways in which we are dominated by disciplinary institutions, for example, then we must also understand the ways in which individuals perform these techniques of domination in ways that can only be expressed through the ways in which individuals act upon themselves. We know this all too well from our experience of disciplinary institutions; we become the good school child by embodying the correct posture, series of responses and practices that are required of us by the disciplinary mechanisms at work within the school, and so on. Equally, though, we must acknowledge that the ways in which we act on ourselves as individuals are 'integrated into structures of coercion or domination' even when we are not always aware of this. We may think that we are doing the right thing by becoming the good school child, with its attendant rewards, but we should not blind ourselves to the domination that operates through such concern with ourselves. In a deliberate echo of his earlier work, and for all that Foucault thinks he has focussed too much on techniques of domination in that earlier work, he stresses that the point of contact between these technologies of domination and the self is 'government' (1997: 154). And, recalling his analysis of power, he says:

Power consists in complex relations: these relations involve a set of rational techniques, and the efficiency of those techniques is due to a subtle integration of coercion-technologies and self-technologies (1997: 155).

This subtle integration is contrasted to the Freudian view that the subject interiorizes the law because this places too much emphasis upon the interior of the subject before its domination. Rather, the subject is constituted through the subtle integration of techniques of domination and techniques of self-constitution that give us our sense of ourselves as beings that have an interior world to which we must be true. It should be clear, therefore, that Foucault's interest in the self in his later work is not the return of the subject but a deeper investigation into its constitution starting, as he says, with techniques of the self rather than techniques of domination, though by no means excluding the latter.

But what are these techniques of the self? We can understand the breadth of what Foucault has in mind, and develop the second sense of technology, by considering the way in which he relates this idea to Heidegger's critique of *techne* and technology. As Foucault understands it, Heidegger thought that it was 'through an increasing obsession with *techne* as the only way to arrive at an understanding of objects' that humanity in the West lost touch with the fundamental question of Being. In a certain sense, Foucault adopts the idea that *techne* has shaped Western thought in the most fundamental manner but he wishes to 'turn the question around and ask which techniques and practices constitute the Western concept of the subject, giving it its characteristic split of truth and error, freedom and constraint' (1997: 152). Rather than assume that technology has led us away from our being-in-the-world and being-with-others, Foucault invites us to think about how technology has shaped our sense of who we are in the world and vis-à-vis others: 'I think it is here that we will find the real possibility of constructing a history of what we have done and, at the same time, a diagnosis of what we are' (1997: 152). In this sense, the stakes of understanding the role of technologies of the self are very high indeed. Foucault's desire to understand the subtle integration of domination and self-constitution in the modern world requires an account of how the Western subject is thoroughly technological from its very inception.

If we have understood the relation of technologies of the self to domination and to the history of Western philosophy then the question still remains:

what are these technologies of the self? While acknowledging that there may be many such technologies of the self that have shaped the Western idea of the subject, Foucault says that those 'directed toward the discovery and the formulation of the truth concerning oneself are extremely important' (1997: 155). These techniques are especially related to the examination of conscience and confession. As with all his genealogical investigations, therefore, his task is to outline how we have come to see confession as intrinsic to the self by first tracking back to a time when we had a different relationship to our self, the epoch of the pagan philosophers. In this way, the complex forces, relations and practices that emerged in Christianity, which constituted our modern sense of the hermeneutics of the self and that persist in psychoanalytical practices of confession, can be traced in ways that reveal their non-natural basis such that we may conceive of ways in which we resist them through modifying their expression in the disciplinary grid of modern institutions.

Drawing out this contrast between the pagan and the Christian technologies of the self, Foucault summarises four key differences. For the pagan philosophers, and he focuses on Seneca, the goal of self-examination is to recall what one has forgotten rather than to discover the truth hidden within oneself, as was the case for the Christians. What one has forgotten, secondly, are the rules by which one should live as opposed to the Christian idea of discovering one's true nature. Thirdly, the recollection of what has been forgotten about the rules of how one should behave is the measure of oneself, whereas in Christianity this measure always has supernatural origins in the word of God. And, lastly, where Christian practices of confession tend toward deciphering the more or less obscure word of God, pagan techniques of self-examination are aimed toward bringing together what one has done and what one should have done, according to a series of external rules. 'We may conclude', Foucault says, 'in ancient philosophy self-examination and confession may be considered a truth-game, and an important truth-game, but the objective of this truth-game is not to discover a secret reality inside the individual' (1997: 164). For all that Christianity employed many of the same techniques as practiced by the Pagan's, the aim was entirely different, the point of the truth-game was different, in that in the hands of the founding fathers of the Church it became a process of self-discovery that revealed the truth about ourselves.

This is not the place to consider the full ramifications of Foucault's genealogy of the modern subject, what it means for our understanding of the classics, of Christian doctrine or contemporary forms of confession such as psychiatry (a good place to start with these investigations would be Martin et al: 1988). These are complicated matters of scholarship worthy of investigation but in the context of this discussion Foucault's point is simple: we may assume that the techniques we employ to know the truth about our nature are in some form natural, but they are not. And, if they have not always been directed toward discovering the truth about our inner nature then they do not need to be directed in this way in the future. Foucault is not inviting us to embrace Pagan practices but in drawing out their difference from Christian techniques of the self he is inviting us to consider what we may do differently now, once we understand how deeply our sense of ourselves as individuals that can decipher our own truth runs within us. In other words, his task is to reveal just how difficult it is to shake off the idea that it is possible to decipher the truth about one's self if one does not direct one's critical attention to this feature of the Western subject. To the extent that it remains unexamined there is always the possibility that investigating the truth about ourselves through confession and its contemporary varieties will return as a form of truth that will be thought unimpeachable and beyond the reach of a politics of truth. Alternatively, to the extent that it is exposed as a question of government, it becomes part of the complex regimes of truth that can be analysed alongside the disciplinary institutions that dominate our modern lives. As such, we can engage in practices of self-examination, technologies of the self, that challenge the idea that we are discovering the truth about ourselves and in so doing engage in practices of resistance precisely at the junction where coercion-technologies and self-technologies converge. In this way, the specific intellectual must not only exchange knowledge at the level of the discursive regime but at the level of our sense of who we are, a task that we can all engage in. The new politics of truth that will emerge is, therefore, also a new politics of the truth about ourselves.

Foucault calls it a new form of 'critical philosophy': 'not a critical philosophy that seeks to determine the conditions and the limits of our possible knowledge of the object, but a critical philosophy that seeks the conditions and the indefinite possibilities of transforming the subject, of transforming ourselves' (1997: 152-3). In bringing this section to a close, it is worth dwelling on just what Foucault means by this. Initially, we can note that he is distancing his version of critical philosophy from Kant's. Rather than presume that we are a subject endowed with certain cognitive apparatuses that enable us to know what we can know and what we will never know, Foucault is inviting us to consider that we are able to transform our very understanding of ourselves in ways that will change how we think about what we know and what we can not know. In this way, the domain of possible knowledge is indefinite rather than limited. Equally, there is a double Kantianism still at play in Foucault's alternative; on the one hand, he still appeals to the need to grasp the conditions that determine the conditioned (in this case, subject) and, on the other hand, we will, once we understand what we can know, without presupposing that this is determined by what we can know now on the basis of how we have been shaped by this Western idea of the subject, know differently. Once liberated from the idea that we are subjects that must know ourselves then there is the possibility of properly acknowledging what we are willing to accept in this world, but also 'to refuse and to change, both in ourselves and in our circumstances' (1997: 152). Taking us back to the guiding themes of this discussion, the truth that will set us free is not a truth that we must find in ourselves if by that we mean a truth that must be deciphered within us, because there is nothing universal and natural about that process itself. Indeed, it is as intimately wrapped up in techniques of domination as is our existence in disciplinary institutions. Rather, a critical philosophy that guides practices of resistance in the name of a new politics of truth should keep in its sights the possibilities for new forms of self-examination, new ways of expressing the relationship we have with our self.

## A Toolbox for Resistance

If Foucault's analyses of the truth-games of self-examination wards off the idea that he returned to the subject or had an idea of constituent subjectivity remaining within his account of the politics of truth, and if it does so because we are able to see that finding out the truth about who we are as critics of society is itself a historically contingent, non-natural and non-universal, idea, then we may say that his later work goes a long way toward Foucault's aim of seeking out and removing the last vestiges of humanism within his project. And yet, it may still appear odd that where this journey has led us is to a version of critical philosophy. Might there still be a surreptitious humanism lurking in the avowed intellectualism of his appeal to critical philosophy? Although we have noted that Foucault's advocacy of the role of specific intellectuals was in response to the Marxist idea of the 'organic intellectual', and although we have seen how his call for a new kind of critical philosophy was rooted in a discussion of the Western ideas of the self, and as such both claims are indubitably context-dependent; there may well be a sense that when pressed about 'what is to be done?' Foucault the intellectual can not help but give an overly prominent role to academic discourse in the practices of resistance that must challenge disciplinary norms. Were this the case then Foucault would be prey to the charge that his position was indeed indebted to a certain hierarchy of knowledge that could not but replay the humanist discourse he tried so vehemently to escape. However, we can see why this is not the case if we return to a mid-period text, the discussion with Deleuze, 'Intellectuals and Power'.

Recorded in 1972, a year after Foucault's debate with Chomsky, these two texts provide the richest and most compelling sources for Foucault's account of the politics of truth. It is appropriate, therefore, as the discussion of Foucault is brought to a conclusion that we turn to the discussion with Deleuze as it neatly summarises Foucault's position and it provides many of the philosophical themes that we can pick up as we delve more deeply into Deleuze's philosophy of difference with a view to sustaining the claims underpinning Foucault's politics of truth. More immediately, though, it provides a compelling account of why it is that a new kind of critical philosophy is not one prey to the charges of intellectualism and surreptitious humanism but is, in fact, a vision of practices of resistance that can be embraced by all. At the heart of the problem, and where the discussion begins, is a novel approach to the relationship between theory and practice.

At Foucault's invitation to explain his allegedly enigmatic relationship to the Maoist politics of the time, Deleuze ventures into a brief but highly influential account of the relationship between theory and practice. There are two standard models of this relationship, he explains. On the one hand, and this is by far the most dominant version, there is the view that practice is 'an application of theory'; on the other hand, and this is more directly related to the Maoist context, there is the view that practice is 'indispensible for the creation of future theoretical forms' (1992b: 205). The former is easily recognisable as that which guides the predominant view that 'the truth will set us free'. If we establish the theoretical claims about the natural world and our nature as human beings first then we will be able to apply these claims forcefully against the systems of domination and oppression that damage our relationship to the world and that prevent our nature from flourishing. Chomsky's radical humanism and anarcho-syndicalism are exemplary in this sense. The latter view of the relationship between theory and practice is less common but nonetheless a stalwart of radical left vanguardism. In many respects, this view harkens back to Marx's famous thesis 11, of his *Theses on Fueurbach*: 'the philosophers have only interpreted the world in various ways; the point is to change it' (2000: 173). Although this gnomic thesis can be read in a number of different ways, it is often taken within Marxism as a claim that the proletariat will lead the way in the revolutionary overthrow of capitalism and in doing so they will create the conditions for a new kind of communist theory. Practices of resistance come first, so to speak, and theoretical invention follows. According to Deleuze, however, whether or not one puts theory or practice first, the result is the same; both positions understand the relationship 'in terms of a process of totalization' (1992b: 205). Exactly what this means is not entirely explained in their discussion but we can infer certain important elements (elements which will then be explored in the next chapter through Deleuze and Guattari's influential discussion of rhizomatics). It is clear, that both versions place one of the terms in a relation of hierarchy vis-à-vis the other; either theory or practice is deemed to have priority and, as such, the privileged term 'totalizes' what is meant by the other. The basis of this totalization is to be found in what we have come to refer to as the idea of the constituent subject; the subject that gives meaning to the world. In the more traditional version, this subject is typically the philosopher understood as the 'great man' able to transcend his social and historical conditions and discern the truth of our nature. In the radical leftist version, this subject is the proletariat, the mass of workers who are able, because of their exploitation and alienation under capitalism, to discern the reality of the capitalist system and provide the grounds for new theoretical innovations by overthrowing it. In both cases, the relationship is one of totalization because the subject is the total guarantor of meaningfulness.

But what other options are there for conceiving of the relationship between theory and practice? The first claim that Deleuze establishes to model an alternative version of this relationship is that 'theory is always local and related to a limited field, and it is applied in another sphere that is more or less distant from it' (1992b: 205). As theories move into these other spheres, however, they encounter 'blockages which require another type of discourse' (1992b: 206) and only if it overcomes these blockages can it move fully into these new domains. This movement, from one domain to another, is a form of practice but equally the practice of accommodating this new set of ideas requires the development of a new theory. The relationship between them, therefore, is not one of 'totalization' but of 'relay': 'Practice is a set of relays from one theoretical point to another, and theory is a relay from one practice to another' (1992b: 206). This image of the relay is compelling and has deep resonances with the idea of the specific intellectual as one who 'exchanges' knowledge, developed later by Foucault (as we noted above). The most important feature of this 'relay' of theory and practice is that it doesn't place one of the terms in a relation of hierarchy to the other. As such, neither theoretician nor the practical activist have priority in assigning meaningfulness to the conditions in which we find ourselves. Rather, they both work on the same level, passing ideas to each other and passing practical responses to each other. Deleuze uses Foucault's creation of the 'information group for prisons, the G.I.P., as a prime example of how this relay can work:

It would be absolutely false to say, as the Maoist implied, that in moving to this practice you were applying your theories. This was not an application; nor was it a project for initiating reforms in the traditional sense. The emphasis was altogether different: a system of relays within a larger sphere, within a multiplicity of parts that are both theoretical and practical (1992b: 206).

The implication is clear; neither theory nor revolutionary practice can claim to contain the conditions within which one can transcend the world in order to know the truth of the situation. Neither the theorist nor the activist can claim to represent the whole, as there is no whole but only a 'multiplicity of parts', a claim that reminds us of Foucault's insistence on the complex and overlapping events that constitute the modern sense of self; from long standing truth games, to local disciplinary regimes of power and knowledge, none of which cohere in a single great battle but which express many forms of combat that must be conducted in many different ways. Dismissing the idea that there is a form of consciousness that can represent the masses, either an intellectual, a union or a group, Deleuze directly tackles the question that, as we have seen in the responses to Foucault's politics of truth, always tend to follow: 'who speaks and acts?' (1992b: 206). His answer is compelling: 'It is always a multiplicity, even within the person who speaks and acts. All of us are "groupuscles"' (1992b: 206).

It is worth drawing out the two key components to this quote. First, there is a direct challenge to the very idea of the constituent subject. In place of the idea of the subject that knows, Deleuze invokes a provocative claim that we, subjects, are always already 'a multiplicity'. This will be explored more fully at the beginning of the next chapter. Second, there is the claim that we are 'groupuscles'. As subjects are already multiplicitous they are already inscribed with elements of the group, but this is not in the sense that we are defined by the groups to which we belong, rather the groups themselves which we express as we speak and act are also multiplicitous. This means that we are the meeting point of our own multiplicity and the multiplicity that constitutes our own sense of self. Giving up on 'totalizing' versions of the relationship between theory and practice, therefore, also means giving up on both individual and collective subjectivities. But if this is the case, then what is it that defines us? In this discussion, Deleuze, in an echo of Nietzsche's claim that doing has priority over being (Nietzsche, 1994: 28), says it is the way we act: 'representation no longer exists, there's only action – theoretical action and practical action which serve as relays and form networks' (1992b: 206-7). Foucault picks up the theme and agrees that we can no longer rely upon the intellectual to 'awaken consciousness', rather it a matter of struggles that must be conducted 'alongside those who struggle for power' in a world in which power operates in often 'invisible and insidious' ways throughout the many domains of disciplinary life and through its institutions. Endorsing Deleuze's characterisation of theory, Foucault says that 'a "theory" is the regional system of this struggle' (1992b: 208).

It is at this point in the discussion that Deleuze provides the titular image for this section: 'Precisely. A theory is exactly like a box of tools' (1992b: 208). There are three aspects to this claim developed by Deleuze. First, he reiterates the idea that theory must give up on all claims to representation; of the world, of our nature, of the masses or individuals oppressed within the world. Theory does not signify anything, or to the extent that theoreticians consider this to be the role of theory they will inevitably create the hierarchies that presume the constituent subject of universal claims to truth. Rather than represent or signify, a theory must be useful, it must have a function in the here and now 'alongside the struggles' or else it will be 'worthless'. Secondly, for a theory to be useful the activity of theorisation itself must be understood as a creative activity. In a deep challenge to the very deeply ingrained idea of the progressive history of philosophy (and science), Deleuze claims that 'we don't revise a theory, but construct new ones' (1992b: 208). The full ramifications of this were not developed until Deleuze and Guattari's (1994) last work together, *What is Philosophy?* Here, however, the implication is that for philosophy to be useful it must co-create in the set of relays it can establish between the multiple individual and the multiple group; that is, at the level of the 'groupuscles' engaged in theoretical and practical activity. Thirdly, such creativity will always be opposed to regimes of power and knowledge because these regimes are always seeking to totalize, whereas creative activity is always engaged in multiplying. We will have cause to examine this claim in more detail in the next chapter. But why do these elements combine to make theory like a box of tools? When we draw them together we can see why. Theories conceived of in this way must be useful in doing something, they must make something from the given materials and they must challenge those existing materials by changing them in new and interesting ways. It is one of the most compelling images of a pragmatist understanding of philosophy in the entire oeuvre, though this also reminds us that it is an idea with a long tradition in the West (and elsewhere).

Thinking about what it means to enact such a creative and practically engaged form of theoretical activity, Deleuze praises Foucault for leading the way. The task is simply not to speak on behalf of others but to let those who suffer from disciplinary institutions speak for themselves. Of course, this would tend towards mirroring the priority of practice over theory if it was understood in a certain way. The point, however, is to dethrone the tendency of theorists to speak for others by first letting people speak for themselves and then engaging in the relays of theory and practice talked about above. In a wonderful example, Deleuze says: 'if the protests of children were heard in kindergarten, if their questions were attended to, it would be enough to explode the entire educational system' (1992b: 209). The point is not to let children take over the kindergartens but to listen to their questions and then to attend to them; this is exactly the relay of theory and practice that will dethrone the constituent subject of both totalizing models of the traditional versions of this relationship.

Pursuing this approach to the relationship between theory and practice has, for both Foucault and Deleuze, immediate implications in terms of the forms of political organisation that can challenge regimes of power and knowledge. As Deleuze puts it, 'we must set up lateral affiliations and an entire system of networks and popular bases' (1992b: 212). And Foucault agrees; 'it is possible that the struggles now taking place and the local, regional, and discontinuous theories that derive from these struggles and that are indissociable from them stand at the threshold of our discovery of the manner in which power is exercised' (1992b: 215). While there is a certain optimism in both claims, an optimism that was not ultimately warranted, the general point is more important: the relay between theory and practice creates the conditions for creative and useful interventions in both domains that will always speak to the here and now, rather than rely upon the 'indignity of speaking for others' (1992b: 209) from a position of the subject who knows the truth.

The image of critical philosophy as a practice of resistance aimed at uncovering and challenging the insidious effects of the politics of truth can now be summarised. From a negative point of view, so to speak, we have journeyed a long way with Foucault (and now Deleuze) to the idea that analysing the deeply entwined nature of power and truth does not necessarily lead to complex scepticism. On this journey, however, we have noted that the risk of dogmatic simplicity lurks deeply within this fabric of power and truth such that one's attempts to unpick it can, at times, lead to stitching regimes of power and knowledge back together if one does not attend to the latent humanism, the latent idea of the constituent subject, that can reside in even one's best attempts to resist the production of truth claims unfettered by politics. From a positive point of view, so to speak, we have found that challenging humanism (and the naturalism and universalism that accompany it) can be articulated in ways that foster practical forms of engagement in the social and political world. These forms of engagement require exchange at the level of discursive regimes, a task for the specific intellectual, but also, and perhaps more so, a relay between intellectuals and activists that is genuinely located on the same plane. This relay must be a genuine practice of learning how to theorise and how to act in many overlapping domains of mutual exchange between groupuscles. In this sense, a politics of truth that aims to resist the ways in which regimes of power and knowledge discipline us into normal human beings is not a grand theory of how these prevent human flourishing, nor a grand revolutionary gesture premised on a utopian vision, but the practice of listening to the small often unheard voices within these disciplinary institutions such that they may be mobilised in new ways of thinking how power operates and new forms of action to change those same institutions. If that sounds like a reformist agenda, it is not. As Deleuze puts it:

The notion of reform is so stupid and hypocritical. Either reforms are designed by people who claim to be representative, who make a profession of speaking for others, and they lead to a division of power, to a distribution of this new power which is consequently increased by a double repression; or they arise from the complaints and demands of those concerned. This latter instance is no longer a reform but revolutionary action that questions (expressing the full force of its partiality) the totality of power and the hierarchy that maintains it (1992b: 208-9).

But giving the last word to Foucault, as we have been guided by his politics of truth thus far, it is important to stress this last point, that the specificity of these struggles does not mean that they do not have a certain kind of generality because 'the generality of the struggle specifically derives from the system of power itself, from all the forms in which power is exercised and applied' (1992b: 217). The important point here is that the generality 'specifically derives' from the system. In this sense, the generality emerges from within the struggle, immanently, and it is this theme of an immanent form of critique and resistance that will be picked up in the next chapter with Deleuze and Guattari.

# Chapter 3: Learning to Resist

What is required of a philosophy of immanent critique and practices of resistance that do not presume the identity of the constituent subject that criticises or resists? In charting Foucault's tireless assault on all forms of humanism (and the modern forms of naturalism and universalism typically associated with it) we have seen how difficult it is to be confident that one has expunged all of its traces from within one's own ideas of critique and resistance. His historian's scepticism to all forms of humanism, including those within traditional and dialectical accounts of history, led him to reflect deeply on the construction of the idea of the human, its effects in terms of knowledge and power and its deep roots within the truth-games of Western philosophy. All the while, he was searching for the overlapping discourses that constituted the human without reifying those discourses themselves, the micro-political moments that can challenge the macro-political revolutionary agendas that have marked modern Western thought and alternatives to the truth-games we use to verify our sense of self; truth-telling regimes that seem so natural to us moderns, but that are in fact just one contingent way of thinking about the truth of who we are as human beings. Questions of theory and practice also came to the fore, and as such, the role of intellectuals and indeed of everyone who, once allowed the dignity to speak for themselves, can provide insight into and alternatives to the disciplinary institutions that dominate our everyday existence. But, perhaps we need to think more expansively about the nature of thought itself, and in so doing cast a wider net around Foucault's scepticism towards humanism by embracing a whole-scale critique of identity per se. Perhaps we can establish forms of practical resistance that manifest this critique of identity whatever the institutional forms that oppress us. It is these tasks that will be explored in this chapter, though only concluded in the final chapter, by turning to Deleuze and Guattari's philosophy of difference and their thoroughgoing pragmatics of creative resistance.

But do we really need to add Deleuze and Guattari into the mix when thinking about how the politics of truth can be both analysed and resisted? There are three broad reasons why it is useful to bring them into the discussion. First, and as we will see in the opening section, Deleuze and Guattari do not begin with a fight against humanism but rather assume that it is no longer relevant so as to engage in the construction of their theoretical and practical work on a radically different basis. Admittedly, by forgetting humanism, rather than fighting against it, their alternative approach can seem so distant from much of what is taken for granted in terms of both critique and resistance that many readers find it difficult to understand, even to begin to find a way into their apparently complex texts. However, the potential it contains, to the extent that their work can and does nonetheless connect to our experience of domination and oppression, is that it has less risk of recuperation within the systems of modern disciplinary institutions so eloquently analysed by Foucault. Secondly, and to the extent that they rail against all identity claims not just those of a humanist variety, the reach of their work is more extensive. In one sense, this is simply the difference between Foucault the historian and Deleuze the philosopher. For Deleuze, there are ways of thinking within Western philosophy so deeply contaminated with presumptions that privilege identity over difference that it is necessary to think about the nature of thought itself, a-historically so to speak, if one is to root out all the risks of recuperation associated with such identity claims. Although by this stage in the argument of this book we may be rightly wary of any a-historical approaches to the extent that they underpin forms of universalism that express the truth about politics rather than the politics of truth, we can now raise the prospect of an a-historical philosophy of difference that does not result in a universal philosophy of identity. Whether or not this philosophical account of difference can then support Foucault's genealogical investigations is a matter of scholarly dispute (Morar et al: 2016); however, as I will present it, the argument is not only that it can, but that it is a necessary support for his investigations into the constituted nature of the modern subject. Thirdly, and in this respect we see the importance of Guattari the activist and analyst every bit as much as Deleuze the philosopher of difference, there is a highly developed account of the relationship between creativity and resistance in their work. We have seen just how important this was for Foucault, for sure; but his emphasis upon the constraints of such creativity within disciplinary institutions led him away from a whole-scale account of the creativity that makes a difference, both theoretically and practically. Theoretically, one of the upshots of focussing instead on Deleuze and Guattari is that we can see just how deeply such creative practices are linked to a metaphysical account of events as significant occurrences; an idea that we will see developed in Deleuze's idea of the encounter that forces us to think. Practically, we will see just how important it is to consider these creative practices of resistance as processes of learning that can unseat all claims to knowledge and the forms of power with which they are imbued. As the chapter title indicates, the result is a more thorough analysis of the immanent critical philosophy with which we ended the last chapter in terms of how we can *learn to resist* the regimes of contemporary institutional life.

## 'Already quite a crowd'

The task of adding Deleuze and Guattari into the mix of Foucault's politics of truth can most usefully begin with one of their most famous, or infamous (depending on your perspective), texts: the 'Introduction: Rhizome' that opens *A Thousand Plateaus: Capitalism and Schizophrenia volume 2* (1987 [1980]). This text has spawned some of the most inspiring work in contemporary critical theory, some of the worst forms of imitation, some of the most insightful philosophical analyses and some of the most vehement critical responses of any philosophical text – Holland (2013) and Adkins (2015) both provide excellent overviews of this text and chart some of the risks as well as benefits of different readings. As we will see below, it is a book that was written to intervene in the world rather than to represent it; and, to this extent, it has certainly succeeded. But there is more to it than a mere series of provocations, and to see why we can begin with its opening lines, which refer to the first volume of *Capitalism and Schizophrenia*: 'The two of us wrote *Anti-Oedipus* together. Since each of us was several, there was already quite a crowd' (1987: 3). We should not underestimate the shock value of these two sentences, nor the philosophical care with which they already express a practically oriented philosophy of difference. The shock comes from the deliberate effacement of their own authorship; it's dissipation into the 'several', and the 'crowd' of which they are simply members. This is not just the familiar claim that all authors have influences, predecessors and inspirations upon which they draw, but the rather more direct claim that, to borrow from Deleuze's discussion from Foucault, each of them as authors was already a 'groupuscle'. The philosophical subtlety comes in the form of presenting from the very beginning this groupuscle as a dynamic authorial assemblage. In the crowd one finds multiple series of dynamic relationships that give movement to their own individual contributions and to the processes of becoming between the two of them as co-authors. What is immediately signalled, therefore, is a process-oriented approach to the construction of *Anti-Oedipus* (1977 [1972]) and by implication *A Thousand Plateaus*, that dethrones the potentially hierarchical role of the author-intellectual as the one that is capable of representing the world and authorised to change it. It is worth giving the rest of this opening paragraph in order to explore these themes further:

Here [in *A Thousand Plateaus*] we have made use of everything that came within range, what was closest as well as farthest away. We have assigned clever pseudonyms to prevent recognition. Why have we kept our own names? Out of habit, purely out of habit. To make ourselves unrecognisable in turn. To render imperceptible not ourselves, but what makes us act, feel, and think. Also because it's nice to talk like everybody else, to say the sun rises, when everybody knows it is only a manner of speaking. To reach, not the point where one no longer says I, but the point where it is no longer of any importance whether one says I. We are no longer ourselves. Each will know his own. We have been aided, inspired, multiplied (1987: 3).

There is a playful, one might even say poetic, rhythm to this opening paragraph that presents a series of provocative and insightful claims that are picked up in the following plateaus of their book. What is within range is both near and far, suggesting that what we are about to read is a book that will traverse disciplinary domains at will, in a similar fashion to the ways in which Foucault speaks of the specific intellectual; there is the continuing use of their own names, and those of others that they draw upon, but only because the habit of using names, especially when linked to books, is so deeply ingrained in our cultural life, not because the designated author has any special authority over the meaning or, as we will see is rather more pertinent, the use of the book; there is an appeal to habit that reaches back into Deleuze's (1991 [1953]) early engagement with Hume and that references the passive syntheses of the self so elaborately outlined in *Difference and Repetition* (1994: Chapter 2); there is a deep concern with both the role of the constituent author and with the need to avoid simply doing away with that role, such that it shouldn't matter if 'one says I', that already signals a profoundly pragmatic approach to such problems; and, a distinct echo of Deleuze's idea of the relay of theory and practice being one in which all such concepts must be multiplied, rather than stultified in necessarily hierarchical regimes of representation.

Moreover, there is a deep concern with the political effects of calling the authorial subject into question. By becoming 'unrecognizable' as authors, as theorists, they will 'render imperceptible' that which conditions their intervention in ways that will enable these conditions to be thought, felt and acted upon by the readers who make use of this book in their own way. As such, the aid and inspiration Deleuze and Guattari have had will, they hope, become an aid and inspiration for others to think, feel and act in ways that relate both to their own existence as a crowd or a groupuscle and in ways that nonetheless embrace their subjective existence as an I that thinks, feels and acts. To this extent, Deleuze and Guattari are already announcing that the often explored tension between the individual and the collective in political movements is one that should be forgotten by remembering that individuals and collectives are both already groupuscles. Moreover, it is important to be 'unrecognisable' because if we begin by re-cognizing their role as authors then we inevitably reconstitute within our analyses the image of cognitive processes that privilege the knowing subject. It is important to be 'imperceptible' because if we perceive them as individuals simply co-authoring a book then we will inevitably reconstitute within our analyses the individualism so central to the forms of capitalism that are co-extensive with this humanist idea of cognition. Equally, while Marx and Engels declared that the proletariat was waiting in the wings to realise its historical mission and overthrow capitalism, Deleuze and Guattari refuse from the outset any idea of a latent revolutionary identity. Instead, they propose that every claim to identity already presupposes a series of movements and transformations that, when released, are the source of multiplying identities and differences beyond even the most radical forms of anti-capitalist politics. The crowd of which they speak is not the proletariat but neither does it exclude them. In fact, the intellectual cannot proclaim the nature of the crowd that will find the means to resist capitalism in advance, because it is never identifiable as One.

But isn't there something odd about all this? They have, after all, written a book rather than forsake the academy in the name of radical political gestures. Why bother writing a book if one has so many problems with authorship? As they make clear, however, the form of this question comes with a series of presuppositions about the relationship between books and the world that they wish to expose and then challenge. Indeed, they say that there are three types of book. The first type is the 'root-book' and this is 'the classical book, as noble signifying and subjective organic interiority...the book imitates the world, as art imitates nature' (1987: 5). The root book is that which contributes to the ever growing tree of human knowledge on the basis of this fundamental imitation: 'the One that becomes two'. The world, the One, is represented in the book, which makes it two. Whether one presumes the originary and timeless status of objects or subjects or both, the world is doubled by this type of classical book through a binary logic that is 'the spiritual reality' of this kind of text. Unsurprisingly, given the opening paragraph, Deleuze and Guattari have little time for this classical book. Their dismissal is immediate: 'nature doesn't work in that way: in nature, roots are taproots with a more multiple, lateral and circular system of ramification, rather than a dichotomous one. Thought lags behind nature' (1987: 5). Of course, to simply state that the classical book fails because 'nature does not work that way' should raise suspicions given our lengthy analyses and rejection of naturalism through Foucault. We will have recourse to specify in the next section just why this claim is not prey to those charges. For now, we can move to the second type of book: that which replaces the root with 'the radicle-system'. This type of book, and they have in mind many of the great modernist experiments in literature, has given up on the possibility of representing the coherent nature of the world on account of the world's intrinsically chaotic nature. Nonetheless, such books remain committed to representing this chaos. As they put it: 'the world has become chaos, but the book remains the image of the world' (1987: 6). It is not enough to do away with the One, to shatter it into fragments, if one then reunifies this fragmented world through the subjective act of authorship. The problem is not just assuming that there is a coherent world to represent, therefore, but that all forms of representation will reconstitute the authority of the constituent author over and above the world they inhabit and in relation to others. What is needed, they argue, is a different kind of book; one that does not presume the unity of the world that can be doubled in a book, nor presume the chaos of the world that can be unified by an author but one in which the chaos of the world can be embraced by the equally chaotic 'crowd' in ways that make it no longer necessary to worry about the unity of the world or of the author. But if the task of writing is not to represent then what is it? According to Deleuze and Guattari, the only point of writing a book is to intervene directly in the world. However, can such a book be written? Can one write a book that intervenes in ways that bring new connections into being, new connections within (rather than over and above) the chaos from within the movement of the crowd (rather than announced by the author)? Their answer is that it can and this form of text is the rhizome book; the book conceived and expressed as a direct intervention into the world of which it is already a part. In order to understand what this might mean we must follow Deleuze and Guattari in their elaboration of the 'approximate characteristics of the rhizome' (1987: 7).

## The multiple must be made!

It was noted above that rather than fight against the humanist grounds of disciplinary institutions (in the style of Foucault) Deleuze and Guattari, in *A Thousand Plateaus*, stake out their a-humanist grounds from the very beginning and then build up a series of claims to create alternatives to traditional practices of resistance that are based on various claims about human nature and the truth about politics. While they are approaching the problem from a different direction, so to speak, Deleuze and Guattari nonetheless face many of the same challenges. In this section we will see how their elaboration of the radical potential of rhizomatics deals with issues of language, naturalism, individualism and collective politics that directly relate to Foucault's discussion with Chomsky. What emerges is a critical method, rhizomatics, that has many similarities with Foucault's idea of genealogy for all that it reaches more directly into the problem of what it means to write (and to think, feel and act) creatively and critically.

Having declared that they do not view *A Thousand Plateaus* as either a classical or modernist book *about* the world, Deleuze and Guattari, with the textual equivalent of a wry smile, say that 'we get the distinct impression we will convince no one unless we enumerate certain approximate characteristics of the rhizome' (1987: 7). If their book is to function as an *intervention* in the world by an authorial crowd that brings new connections between ideas and action into existence, then we need to know what a rhizome is, and how it functions. Simply put, a rhizome is a continuously growing stem that runs laterally underground, usually just under the surface. In contrast to the root, which is the anchor of the plant structure, the rhizome puts out shoots and then establishes roots at certain advantageous points. We will see how this relationship between rhizome and root (and therefore, the tree structures that the root supports) is important as Deleuze and Guattari develop this image of the rhizome. But, for now, it is useful simply to reconstruct their philosophical elaboration of the characteristics of rhizomes. They provide six such characteristics described as principles, with the first and second, fifth and sixth presented as pairs.

The first pair of principles are these: 'principles of connection and heterogeneity: any point of a rhizome can be connected to anything other, and must be' (1987: 7). Elaborating upon what they mean by these two principles it is telling that they contrast them with the 'linguistic tree on the Chomsky model' (1987: 7). Whereas Chomsky's approach to language, as we saw above, begins with the idea that there are shared universal features of language innate to human beings, from which all creative language use stems, Deleuze and Guattari argue that 'Chomsky's grammaticality, the categorical S symbol that dominates every sentence, is more fundamentally a marker of power than a syntactic marker' (1987: 7). This reminds us of Foucault's claim that Chomsky's idea of linguistic creativity is deeply embedded within humanist regimes of knowledge and power. But, in the hands of Deleuze and Guattari, this claim is given a novel twist: 'our criticism of these linguistic models is not that they are too abstract but, on the contrary, that they are not abstract enough, that they do not reach the *abstract machine* that connects a language to the semantic and pragmatic contents of statements, to collective assemblages of enunciation, to a whole micropolitics of the social field' (1987: 7). Although Foucault did not put it like this, in part because of his genealogical wariness toward abstraction, it does nonetheless point to the role of language within the grid of modern disciplinary societies (the difference between 'grid' and 'abstract machine' pointing to a different legacy of structuralism within the respective projects). Where they certainly agree is that Chomsky's model does little to express the idea that language 'evolves by subterranean stems and flows' like a rhizome that connects its heterogeneous nature to non-linguistic operations, such as those one finds in 'a parish, a bishopric, a capital' (1987: 7). Importantly, therefore, thinking of language in this way provides a method for the connection of any statement to anything else, anything other than language that establishes the roots of linguistic meaning. As they say, 'a method of the rhizome type...can analyse language only by decentering it onto other dimensions and registers' (1987: 8). We will never understand linguistic creativity, therefore, solely in terms of grammaticality and innate human characteristics. Rather, linguistic creativity is the result of the ways in which language is expressed within systems of power, those 'other dimensions and registers', that determine what counts as meaningful.

The third principle of the rhizome is the principle of multiplicity: 'it is only when the multiple is effectively treated as a substantive, "multiplicity", that it ceases to have any relation to the One as subject or object, natural or spiritual reality, image and world' (1987: 8). We have noted the presence of this and related terms since the beginning of this discussion, especially the persistent return of the idea that the task of theory and practices of resistance is not to represent reality but to multiply it. In this principle of rhizomatics we have the philosophical claim underpinning these evocations. They put it like this: 'a multiplicity has neither subject nor object, only determinations, magnitudes, and dimensions that cannot increase in number without the multiplicity changing in nature' (1987: 8). The first part of this claim means that multiplicities do not have 'points or positions' such as those found within 'a structure, tree, or root' (1987: 8). The second part means that without such anchors the nature of multiplicities can be transformed; they can multiply, and in multiplying become radically transformed, through changes in intensity. In this we find an expression of what happens when something significant happens; that is, when we are in the midst of an event. When something significant happens within a multiplicity, such as the language of 'the parish' becoming recoded within the language of 'the capital', we have a change of intensity that changes the nature of the multiplicity itself. Charting these events is one of the key practices of rhizomatics as a method for the analysis of difference rather than identity. Once again, it reminds us of Foucault's account of the movements between overlapping and superimposed domains and, just as this led Foucault to adumbrate the idea of the disciplinary grid of modern societies, so Deleuze and Guattari generalise this idea when they say that all multiplicities invoke a 'plane of consistency' (1987: 9). And, in another echo of Foucault, and the structuralism they all share, they say that 'the plane of consistency (grid) is the outside of all multiplicities' (1987: 9). Changes in intensity within and between multiplicities, therefore, increase the number of connections that exist on the plane; both as a ramification of the power systems they imply and as a challenge to those very systems of power. Knowing which is which is possible, as we will see, but only in a pragmatic rather than a definitive sense.

The fourth principle is that of 'asignifying rupture'. Reminding us that rhizomes are not just part of the anatomy of plants but that they function across the biological domain, they say that 'you can never get rid of ants because they form an animal rhizome that can rebound time and again after most of it has been destroyed' (1987: 9). The idea here is that because there is no unity at the root of the rhizome system, because it functions as a multiplicity, it always has the possibility to forge new connections in new territories. While the remains of the ant colony scuttle off to find a new home so they leave one territory to create a new one, a process that Deleuze and Guattari refer to as de- and re- territorialization. However, given the fact that this requires a change of intensity, it is clear that the ant colony will not be the same multiplicity as that which it was in its old territory. It will be engaged in a process of becoming in relation to the outside forged within the new territory – the bigger hill, the deeper lake, the presence of different animals and humans and so on. There is, in other words, a rupture involved that does not signify anything. Importantly for this discussion, Deleuze and Guattari link these processes of territorialisation to the relationship between the book and the world: 'the book is not an image of the world. It forms a rhizome with the world...the book assures the deterritorialization of the world, but the world effects a reterritorialization of the book, which in turn deterritorializes itself in the world (if it is capable, if it can)' (1987: 11). The punch line is in the brackets: plenty writers think that they have written books that will change the world only to find their work recuperated back within the structures they fought so hard against. Only a book that has the process of de- and re- territorialisation embedded within its internal logic can hope to ward off this recuperative machinery. Only a book that is in a relation of becoming with the world can express its character as a multiplicity, critically. And the same can be said of all who think, feel and act in ways to change the world: if the thinking, feeling and acting of individuals and groups do not break out into new territories through connections that rupture with the past then they will always tend to 'contain microfascisms waiting to crystallize' (1987: 10).

This leads neatly onto the last pair of principles as they express practical ways of avoiding the crystallization of such microfascisms: the principles of cartography and decalcomania. Cartography, here, is understood as the creative and productive process of mapping a territory in contrast to the representational and reproductive practice of tracing. The rhizome, they say, is 'a map not a tracing' (1987: 12). The point of a map is not that it gives an exact representation of reality but that it is constructed in ways that enable us to function in the world; it is useful. The map, as they say, 'has to do with performance', how we move around a territory and it can do so through 'multiple entryways, as opposed to the tracing, which always comes back "to the same"' (1987: 12). But having established the practice of mapping as a crucial feature of rhizomatic method they then present one of the most important but overlooked features of this method. They reflect on whether or not mapping is 'good' and tracing 'bad'. They are clear: it would be a mistake to think this because the 'tracings should always be put back on the map' (1987: 13). This is the principle of decalcomania, the art of transferring a design. Just as one creates the map to enable one's movement, so one must also trace one's steps to see where one has arrived. The point, though, is not to see the tracing as the reality of the map but to 'plug' the tracing back into the map such that it can be used to create a new series of movements. A new series will follow because the art of transferring a tracing on to a map is 'nonsymmetrical' to that of map making: 'if it is true that it is of the essence of the map or rhizome to have multiple entryways, then it is plausible that one could even enter them through tracings or the root-tree, assuming the necessary precautions are taken' (1987: 14). The contrast, therefore, between the rhizome and the tree must not become the subject of a normative overcoding but the source of a pragmatics of 'composing multiplicities, or aggregates of intensity' (1987: 15). As such, tracings are not in themselves 'bad'; indeed, to map the normative categories of good and bad onto rhizome and root/tree respectively will simply reproduce the structures of power and knowledge that the method of rhizomatics aims to destabilize and decentre. It is always, as they say several times throughout this introductory chapter, a matter of method; 'to attain the multiple one must have a method that effectively constructs it' (1987: 22). It is not a method, however, that will guide us to legitimate forms of knowledge or truth. In the hands of Deleuze and Guattari, rhizomatics is a method to assess a pragmatics of movement and becoming in order to think, feel and act differently in the world and, therefore, of making new worlds. Rather than a guide to the operation of a universal subject capable of knowing the world as it is, rhizomatics is a method for bringing the subject and the world into a process of mutual becoming such that both can be differently constituted.

Two further issues must be addressed now that we have outlined the philosophical principles of the rhizome. First, for all that rhizomatics as method is not a form of humanism, it does seem to rest upon a form of naturalism in the sense that it appears to draw its inspiration from botany in the construction of its principles. Secondly, for all that rhizomatics is a way of thinking methodically, it is not yet clear that it can actually establish a basis for critique as a practical and not merely scholarly or intellectual activity. These two issues blend together in important respects.

Regarding the first of these, there is a lingering tendency within applied Deleuzism to treat rhizomes as a thing in the world (the social, cultural, psychosexual, economic worlds and so on, as well as the natural world) that must simply be discovered by the researcher and/or activist in order that the complicated networks underpinning all claims to identity can be exposed and then regimes of knowledge and power challenged. This would be a mistake. It is a mistake because it replicates the Chomskyian model of the truth about politics that we have left behind in the first chapter. It would be a mistake because it repeats the representational gesture at the heart of humanist philosophies and all philosophies that privilege identity over difference. To the extent that it remains a representational gesture, rhizomatics will inevitably rest upon and reconstitute those same structures of knowledge and power that one is seeking to expose. Rather, it is important to state as clearly as possible that these principles of the rhizome are outlined in order to forge a new *method for intervening in the world in both theory and practice* and, in this sense, it is always better to talk of rhizomatics rather than to veer too near toward the danger of assuming that rhizomes can be represented as natural and good (and all else bad). It is with this in mind that one can see that the most important claim in the whole of their introduction is that 'the multiple must be made' (1987: 5). It cannot simply be represented. The construction of the multiple helps steer us away from naturalising rhizomes as the underlying truth of our existence and it reminds us that there is always practical and creative work to be done in exposing the arborescent structures of knowledge and power within which we find ourselves.

But how does one make the multiple? Their answer is two-fold. First, 'subtract the unique from the multiplicity to be constituted' (1987: 5); second, subtract 'the One' from all multiplicities (1987: 21). Both techniques amount to the same thing; just from different directions, so to speak. When looking to enact a rhizomatic method one must focus on the unique, the singular entity (not necessarily an individual but it could be) that stands out as different, then ensure that one's analysis of this difference is not reconstituted into an overarching identity reapplied to the group. In both cases, one can make the multiple methodically by operating at 'n-1 dimensions', where the '1' is both the unique and the overarching identity that must be subtracted in order to retain the uniqueness of the entity and the dynamics of the assemblage. In stark contrast to a whole raft of modern methods that focus on generalizability, rhizomatics brings to our attention the unique movements and changes in intensity that transform the nature of assemblages by mapping the connections that are forged on the plane of consistency (Foucault's disciplinary grid being a version of this plane, that accounts for the superimposition of modern discourses of knowledge and power). In this way, rhizomatics always operates from 'the middle', the middle of a movement from the assemblage to its outside, where this movement itself is defined as a change in intensity. As Deleuze and Guattari put it, there are no origins and ends, only lines and movements. Moreover, it is these movements that bring forth the titular idea of the plateau in A Thousand Plateaus: 'we call a plateau any multiplicity connected to other multiplicities by superficial underground stems in such a way as to form or extend a rhizome' (1987: 22). The plateaus that connect rhizome to rhizome, that are constructed through the extension of a rhizome by intensification, are always in the middle of assembled structures of knowledge and power. Rhizomatics directs our methodological gaze to these plateaus, to the surface of the middle where the movements occur. This method, thereby, respects the uniqueness of the movement and its capacity to change the assemblage from which it has emerged (and to keep doing so as it is reterritorialized, 'if it can'). For all that this will be specified further below, it is possible at this stage to say that the task of practices of resistance that can avoid such reterritorialization is to make the multiple, to forge new multiplicities that establish new plateaus on which to move in and around and through and beyond systems of knowledge and power.

But doesn't this still rely upon a view of thinking itself that has priority over that which is thought about? Is there not still the possibility that a method that focuses on unique shifts of intensity relies too heavily upon a traditional image of what it means to think? Is there not a reasonable concern lurking within this view of rhizomatics that it gives priority to creative thought over and above practical political activism? There are these dangers, and they have been picked up by the critical literature, as we will see in the next chapter when we turn to Badiou's (2000 [1997]) critical response to Deleuze's philosophy of multiplicity and difference. However, in their introduction to *A Thousand Plateaus*, Deleuze and Guattari argue that rhizomatics presumes that 'thought is not arborescent, and the brain is not a rooted or ramified matter' (1987: 15). For all that 'many people have a tree growing in their heads... the brain itself is much more a grass than a tree' (1987: 15). And here we see that Deleuze and Guattari have, in one sense, followed Foucault in taking the cognitive structures identified by Kant outside of the head, into a realm of dynamic and changing structures that they call multiplicities, but only to then return them inside the head once their radically connective and heterogeneous nature has been established. In this way, what we come to know about the world can only be established through a rhizomatic process of making the multiple, where this multiplicity exists both inside and outside the head, so to speak. Subtracting the unique and refusing identity operate in both places at once because there is no significant difference between them. In this sense, Deleuze and Guattari's rhizomatics is a form of naturalism but one which also embraces the idea that the transcendental conditions of the formation of knowledge about the world are not centred within the subject but decentered across the connections between brain and world, individual and group. As such, while they share with other naturalists (such as Chomsky) a desire to do away with any supernatural claims, they do not take naturalism to imply either the privilege of the natural sciences in the formation of knowledge nor do they privilege the constituent subject implied by giving the natural sciences epistemological priority. Deleuze used the term transcendental empiricism to designate this revised Kantianism and we can see what it means for our understanding of critique as we turn to the next section on what it means to learn to think differently. By way of a last word on rhizomatics and a first word on transcendental empiricism it is worth closing this chapter on what Deleuze and Guattari call the 'important point':

...the root-tree and canal-rhizome are not two opposed models: the first operates as a transcendent model and tracing, even if it engenders its own escapes; the second operates as an immanent process that overturns the model and outlines a map, even if it constitutes its own hierarchies...We employ a dualism of models only in order to arrive at a process that challenges all models (1987: 20).

This process has a deceptively everyday name; learning.

## Learning to Think Differently

At every turn, Deleuze and Guattari begin with processes, movements and multiplicities. The rhizome is an image of how these movements work in the world, criss-crossing multiplicities on the plateaus these movements establish, but it is also an image of how we think about these movements in the world. It is never enough to make the world complex while grounding knowledge of that complexity in the constituent subject. This was Kant's tactic, as we saw above, and it resides to this day in all forms of humanism, no matter how radical they appear. For all the intricate nature of the cognitive apparatuses that he discerned within the subject, the overall effect was to regulate the world through the subject's ordering of it in the process of cognition. This is what he meant by critical philosophy. But if we give up on the task of legitimating the limits of knowledge through the subject then do we have to give up on the project of a critical philosophy that can challenge the dangerous effects of the illegitimate regimes of knowledge and power that dominate our lives? We have noted, in the previous section, that Deleuze and Guattari see rhizomatics as a method that can bring the multiplicitous nature of the world and thought into connection, in a process oriented manner. But does operating between these multiplicities, from the middle, mean that we have to give up on the hope of establishing grounds for knowledge and thereby give up on the prospect of forms of critique that might animate practices of resistance? In this section, we shall see that Deleuze's philosophy of difference is a critical philosophy of a particular, immanent, kind. In the next section, we will explore how he understood this in terms of resistance.

Deleuze's most elaborate response to the idea of critique is given in the chapter on 'The Image of Thought' in *Difference and Repetition* (although an equally important text in this regard would be *Nietzsche and Philosophy*, both of which come to the same conclusions). This is a formidable chapter not least because he charts a series of ways in which philosophers of widely differing positions, not just those in the critical tradition, have struggled with the fundamental question of how to begin in philosophy. This problem of beginnings in philosophy, as he says, is fundamentally a question of what it means to think. In these terms, each of the different philosophers he considers provide an image of thought that establishes and motivates their systematic projects. For all that there is variety in these projects, Deleuze claims that they all cohere around a certain form of philosophical dogmatism. The dogmatic is the image philosophers often create of what it means to think within their respective systems that cannot itself be subject to criticism, even within the most critical philosophies. This dogmatism is unpacked by way of a number of philosophical postulates; eight in total. At the end of the chapter Deleuze presents the eighth postulate, the postulate of knowledge, as the 'one which incorporates and recapitulates all the others in a supposedly simple result' (1994: 167). Simply put, this eighth postulate is the idea that the point of thinking is 'to know'; it is 'the postulate of the end, or result' (1994: 167). The claim here is striking: if we presume that the point of thinking is 'to know' (the world, ourselves, how we relate to each other and so on) then we will, necessarily according to Deleuze, engage in forms of philosophical dogmatism. First principles, those that guide our image of what it means to think, will be deemed to be beyond critique and they will, therefore, reconstitute regimes of knowledge and power that seek to stifle movement and becoming. But, it is important to be clear, Deleuze is not calling to account this dogmatism in the name of 'not-knowing'; he is not proposing a form of scepticism that simply refuses all claims to knowledge. As we have noted from the very beginning of this book, such a position will rob us of any power to resist the dogmatic regimes that discipline our existence. But how does one critique the very idea of 'critique as the task of establishing the legitimate limits of knowledge' without falling into scepticism and powerlessness? As we saw at the end of the last section, Deleuze and Guattari's approach is not to oppose models, except for the pragmatic effect of rendering them as moments in a continuous process. In this way, Deleuze's approach to the critique of critique is not to abandon it in favour of some other approach but to get inside the claim of what it means to know and explore that which conditions our pursuit of knowledge; his project is a critique of critique *from within*, so to speak. Searching for the conditions of the postulate of knowledge means that Deleuze's philosophy is still a critical one, it is still searching for the transcendental basis of knowledge but, as we will see, what makes a difference in his approach is that he does not ground this transcendental analysis in a transcendent object or subject, rather in movements and processes that are neither objective nor subjective but constitutive of both. It is this sense of the constituted nature of objects and subjects that he takes from his particular interpretation of empiricism and, when combined with the search for the conditions of knowledge, gives his distinctive and highly original philosophical project the title 'transcendental empiricism'. For thorough explorations of what is meant by this apparently oxymoronic term see Williams (2003), de Beistegui (2010) and Smith (2012). For us, the importance of this innovative project is that it seeks to adumbrate a properly immanent approach to critical philosophy that may establish the theoretical claims embedded within practices of resistance that can sustain themselves against the tendency to become recuperated within systems of knowledge and power.

We can explore what he means by this if we take the example of learning to swim, an example he uses at the end of his chapter. There is no doubt that as we embark on learning to swim that we are guided by the idea that we want to know how to swim. But, equally, we are aware that we will never learn to swim by simply reading the manuals, no matter how intricate the account of swimming they contain. In order to learn to swim we must bring our body into contact with a body of water and, also, the bodies of knowledge contained within the manuals or given by an instructor. It is the 'conjugation' of these different bodies that will enable learning. As Deleuze puts it: 'to learn to swim is to conjugate the distinctive points of our bodies with the singular points of the objective idea [of the sea] in order to form a problematic field' (1994: 165). This might sound like a rather overblown philosophical account of something that is rather mundane but it is important to dwell on what he means in more detail to see why it is necessary to think in these terms. The conjugation in question is that of bringing the particularities of our bodies, the length of our arms, their rigidity or flexibility and so on, into connection with the waves and modulations of the water within which we are trying to swim. As we embrace this conjugation we may think that we are finding a solution to the problem of swimming but in fact what we find is that we are engaged in a process of continuously discerning what the problem is (if I move my arm in this way then the water responds in that way, and so on). What we find, therefore, is that we are embedded within a problematic field rather than simply solving the problem by applying a ready-made solution to the question of how to swim. This becomes acute as we try to swim more efficiently, or in different kinds of water, or competitively, or for fun with the kids. Nonetheless, what we experience is that we learn to swim in these different contexts without even really thinking about how to swim, we are learning without knowing through the continuous conjugation of our body with that of the water and with the body of swimming knowledge that we have acquired through experience and/or through the manuals and instructor. For all that are in continuous interaction with what we know, therefore, we are also engaged in a continuous process of learning that changes what we know. (Referring to the previous section, we can say that we are always mapping our relationship to the territory of the water, but then also tracing what we have learned back on to this map, and this will be productive only to the extent that we are willing to plug what we know back into learning in the new body of water we encounter, or when we find that swimming with a broken arm requires a new series of bodily movements, and so on.) Deleuze summarises it this way: 'learning always takes place in and through the unconscious, thereby establishing a profound complicity between nature and mind' (1994: 165). The important point here is two-fold. Not only do we engage in a practice of learning before we can claim to know, but when we do think we know we must be open to learning again as we encounter different situations. Knowledge, therefore, does not condition learning, rather learning conditions knowledge because, 'we never know in advance how someone will learn' (1994: 165).

This has important consequences for our understanding of critique: 'it is from learning, not from knowledge, that the transcendental conditions of thought must be drawn' (1994: 166). If we presume that critique is aimed at establishing what we can know, legitimately, then we are already privileging the idea of the end of knowledge and the constituent subject (be it the philosopher or, as we noted above, the revolutionary proletarian subject) that will ground that end. But if we acknowledge that all forms of knowledge must be learned, and all learning requires the intricate conjugation of 'nature and mind', of our bodies with that of other bodies, then we must acknowledge that there is no way of knowing in advance what will count as legitimate, what the end will be, who will learn and how. Each of these components must be extracted from the image we have of what it means to think and from the image we have of who we think is capable of thinking. Once extracted, all we have left in place of these is the different forms of movement within and between bodies that enables learning; movements can only be accounted for in terms of the difference they make to what we know, rather than in terms of legitimating what counts as knowledge. In this sense, 'learning is the true transcendental structure which unites difference with difference' (1994: 166-7). Whereas Kant 'seemed equipped to overturn the image of thought' (1994: 136) he did in fact create a legislative structure in order to judge what counts as knowledge and what does not. As such, as Deleuze puts it, 'critique has everything – a tribunal of justices of the peace, a registration room, a register – except the power of a new politics which would overthrow the image of thought' (1994: 137). And, without this power of a new politics, Kantian critique will always amount to 'tracing' the empirical on to the transcendental rather than provide a 'properly transcendental empiricism' (1994: 143). To challenge the world which we experience we need the power of the new politics that will dispense with Kant's judicial and legislative image of critique in favour of an alternative critical philosophy based upon the idea that learning is the condition for the creation of knowledge: 'the conditions of a true critique and a true creation are the same: the destruction of an image of thought which presupposes itself and the genesis of the act of thinking in thought itself' (1994: 139). All forms of thought that presuppose what it means to think must be destroyed and they can be by learning how to think for your self, where your 'self' is the 'groupuscle' in which it no longer matters whether or not one says I.

But is there not a lurking concern that this emphasis on learning may simply repeat the problem of grounding critique in a subject, this time a subject who learns, no matter how complicated this subject appears to be? As the example of swimming makes clear, however, it is not the subject or the groupuscle that conditions learning but the learning that conditions the formation of a 'subjective' groupuscle: 'something in the world forces us to think' (1994: 139). What is this something? In *Difference and Repetition*, Deleuze calls it 'an encounter'. What is an encounter? It is important to specify that not all bodily interactions (of our body with the body of water, for example) force us to think; many, it would seem, simply reconstitute what we know about ourselves. Stepping into the sea, for example, may confirm for me that I do not like being in the water. This is a process of recognition: we re-cognize what we know about ourselves in an act of confirming what we already know. However, this bodily interaction becomes an encounter if we 'let go' of what we know about ourselves in order to sense what is happening to us. In recognition, that which 'bears directly upon the senses' (the lapping waves, for example) is treated as object 'which can be recalled, imagined or conceived' (I didn't like the lapping of waves at my feet as a child and I don't like it now). But, Deleuze claims, sensation itself 'is opposed to recognition' because that which is sensed exists in the profound complicity of nature and mind, and not simply in the mind of the subject. What we sense, in other words, is not the unitary thing we call water, but its intricate movements around our feet, and what we think of as the movement of our feet is in fact a series of intricate vibrations and responses to this movement of the water. Between the two there is an intensity that neither exists in the world nor in the subject but between the two. It is an intensity that Deleuze refers to as 'the being of the sensible' (1994: 140) because it is what makes sensation possible in the first place. Colloquially, we might say that 'letting go' of our desire to place this intense sensation within our already established register of what we like and don't like will enable us to experience the possibility for learning that it contains. But this only makes sense if we are careful not to reintroduce a subjective control over this process and it is for this reason that Deleuze often refers to the encounter as a violent process, one in which our sense of what we know about ourselves is shaken and the neat juridical apparatuses of our mind is brought into a state of discordance. In this violent encounter, however, we experience thought: 'it is always by means of intensity that thought comes to us' (1994: 144). In relation to Kant, this has two key consequences. First, it means that 'the transcendental is always answerable to a superior empiricism which alone is capable of exploring its domain and its regions' (1994: 143). Secondly, intensity brings the faculties into discord rather than harmony in ways that mean that each of the faculties we recognise as belonging to humans (the faculty for language, imagination and such like) are not the only one's that may exist. As Deleuze speculates, there are 'faculties yet to be discovered, whose existence is not yet even suspected' (1994: 143). We will only bring these into existence through processes of learning conditioned by intensive encounters with others; the world, other people individually and/or collectively, animals, and so on. This helps us to deepen our sense of the creativity that Deleuze has in mind as 'to think is to create' does not only mean that we are beings capable of imagining new ways of being in the world, it means that 'to create is first of all to engender 'thinking' in thought' (1994: 147). In this latter case, we see that Deleuze is open to new ways of thinking and new ways of thinking about the world. Both are possible through learning, if learning is understood as a fundamental encounter with something that forces us to think. However, there are two further aspects to explore if we are to bring this immanent critique into contact with the idea of a politics of truth. First, we must consider the relationship between the encounter that conditions learning and the idea of event. Secondly, we must assess what this all means for the concept of truth.

Throughout the discussions of Foucault in the previous two chapters, we noted that he was both critical of Chomsky's idea of a revolutionary event and that he developed an account of the complex overlapping and superimposed events that constituted the modern subject, which are amenable to genealogical investigation. Both of these challenged the traditional forms of resistance based on alleged truths about human nature and our political situation. Nonetheless, they did so in an external manner, so to speak. For all that these complex overlapping events make it difficult to sustain the idea that there is a universal human nature, devoid of political interest, that can serve as the basis for legitimate resistance to oppressive regimes, Foucault's account does not, in itself, provide a way of articulating a more internal relationship between critique and events. This is what we find in Deleuze. The encounter that conditions learning brings the idea of the event into the heart of the creation of knowledge. One immediate consequence is that this provides a way of thinking about how we can critique all claims 'to know' that deny their own conditions (opinions) in a manner similar to Kant's critical project, and those that account for their conditions with reference to a transcendent subject (dogmatism), in a manner that critiques Kant's critical project itself. This does not mean that we refuse all claims to knowledge but that these claims can only meet the Kantian test of critical philosophy by acknowledging that they are conditioned by encounters in the world that force us to think in ways that we call learning. As such, these events always contain the possibility that we may be able to think differently – not just differently about the same things but differently in the sense that we may 'discover' or better yet create new faculties of cognition. When we think about the conditions of critique, Deleuze says, we must view the condition as a 'condition of real experience, not of possible experience. It forms an intrinsic genesis, not an extrinsic conditioning' (1994: 154). In learning we find the unavoidably empirical conditions of a properly transcendental account of what we can know. The upshot is a philosophical justification for immanent critique.

But what does this mean for the idea of truth? As Deleuze puts it: 'In every respect, truth is a matter of production, not of adequation' (1994: 154). In Foucault's closing theses in *Truth and Power* we noted that he was by no means averse to talking about harnessing 'the power of truth'. To this extent, truth could still play a role in critique and practices of resistance, if it is conceived as a truth that has a pragmatic rather than absolute basis to it. Deleuze sums it up like this:

> We always have as much truth as we deserve in accordance with the sense of what we say. Sense is the genesis or the production of the true, and truth is only the empirical result of sense. We rediscover in all the postulates of the dogmatic image the same confusion: elevating a simple empirical figure to the status of a transcendental, at the risk of allowing the real structures of the transcendental to fall into the empirical (1994: 154).

On the one hand, this deflates the idea of truth to which we commonly adhere. Truth is not about constructing a proposition that is adequate to that which we think we already know about the world or about ourselves. On the other hand, truth is not rejected completely. As that which is produced, through our sensory engagement with the world in encounters that condition learning, truth can be maintained as an empirical result of the new worlds, and new ways of knowing the world, that we establish in such encounters. Of course, these are not fixed truths, universal and timeless, rather they are truths that emanate from encounters and as such are always perspectival and open to transformation. The truth still has a role to play, it still has power within a thorough going immanent critique and politics of truth, but this power is only maintained if the sense of the encounter is maintained. But this sense cannot be maintained if we treat it as either a thing of this world or as a feature of the knowing subject; rather, it operates intensively within the complicity of nature and mind such that 'it is always by means of an intensity that thought comes to us' (1994: 144). What does this mean for our understanding of resistance?

## R is for Resistance

There is no doubt that the idea of resistance has an ambiguous role in Deleuze's philosophy of difference. As we have noted in previous chapters, there are moments when Deleuze embraces the idea of resistance, as in his conversation with Foucault. Moreover, it has a significant presence throughout his oeuvre, from *Nietzsche and Philosophy* (1986 [1962]) to the posthumously aired interview with Claire Parnet 'From A to Z' (2012), which includes a lengthy episode entitled 'R is for Resistance' (to which we will return below). And yet, it is also clear that Deleuze always maintained a cautious attitude to this idea. This caution is most evident in his reflections on Foucault. In his book *Foucault* (1988), but also in a series of short texts and interviews, he conveys doubts about the role of resistance in Foucault's oeuvre (Deleuze: 1995). To a certain extent the difference in attitude toward resistance he discerns between himself and Foucault is a result of their different theoretical starting points. As we have noted, Foucault begins with analyses of the regimes of knowledge and power that have shaped our sense of ourselves and in so doing the idea of resistance to these has a systematic role. Deleuze, on the other hand, tends to focus on what is required of a fully-fledged philosophy of difference such that resistance to those institutions that constrain us in certain identities are epiphenomenal and, therefore, resistance to them is less central. Deleuze, one might say, likes to forget that identity matters and then engage in constructive theorising, whereas Foucault likes to remind us that our identities are always constructed and then resist the institutions that determine our 'nature'. That said, there is rather more to it as we consider the ambiguous role of resistance in Deleuze's oeuvre.

The first additional point to consider is his relationship with Guattari. While it is too simple to suggest that Guattari brought the activism into their partnership, it does express some of the dynamic between them. Their first book together, *Anti-Oedipus*, was described by Deleuze as a 'book of political philosophy'. Their second book together, *Kafka: Towards a Minor Literature* (1986 [1975]) was a political as opposed to psychoanalytic reading of Kafka's work. We have also seen how their third major work, *A Thousand Plateaus*, sets in motion of a political challenge to authorship and authority from the very beginning; themes developed across the various plateaus, though most explicitly in '1227, Treatise on Nomadology – The War Machine' and '7000 BC, Apparatus of Capture'. However, by the time of their last major collaboration, *What is Philosophy?*, it seemed that politics had drifted out of sight, apparently relegated to some rather cursory remarks about utopianism. If it is the case that Deleuze had rather more of a hand in the authorship of this last work than Guattari, then this might seem to confirm that Deleuze's interests were always rather more philosophical than political, hence the equivocations that can be discerned with regard to the idea of resistance.

Attributing such a distinction between Deleuze and Guattari is rather unsatisfactory, however. It does not, in the first instance, give due regard to the idea that their co-authorship was a process of becoming between them and their various interlocutors; Dosse (2010: 14-15, and throughout) gives a nuanced account of their authorial relationship. Equally, it does not really address the problem of the political in their work to its fullest extent. We can summarise the main problem: in the absence of a fully worked out political philosophy, an absence that speaks to their wariness of any political position that identifies the problem only to then offer the solution to that problem, is there a structural weakness in their equally clear opposition to forms of domination because it lacks a justification for practices of resistance? To see what this structural weakness might be, and why it might not be such a weakness, we need to pick up where we left off in the previous section with the ideas of critique and creativity.

What is the relationship between a philosophy of immanent critique and practices of resistance? It was noted above (Chapter 2) that Deleuze sees an intrinsic relationship between theorising and resistance: Deleuze 'fully agrees' with Foucault that 'theory is by nature opposed to power' (1992b: 208). Such theorising, we can now say, is the kind of creative response to an encounter with the outside that engenders 'thinking within thought'. Bringing these elements together, we are now in a position to articulate the relationship between critique and resistance simply: to create is to resist. Equally, however, we can now appreciate the complexity of this simple statement. On the side of critique, so to speak, we can now understand that the learning process that is the 'true condition of critique' is a fundamentally creative activity. The critique of all philosophical systems that are driven by the desire 'to know', the critique of critique, is expressed through practices of learning how to think differently. However, these practices of learning are not consigned to the minds of the philosophers or any other subject, individual or collective. Rather they are located within the 'profound complicity of nature and mind' that we noted above. Learning is a process that begins with a violent shock to what we think we know, a shock that comes in the form of an encounter with the outside, where this outside is both external to the assemblages within which we are defined and the discord of the faculties that shape our sense of what we know. In order to learn, therefore, we must find new ways of expressing the 'profound complicity between nature and the mind'; that in-between zone of intensity where 'difference unites with difference'. These new modes of expression are always a particular and creative response to the impossibility of incorporating the shock to the system within what we think we already know. In this sense, there is no creativity in general, for all that creativity expresses, what I have referred to previously as, the idea of pure critique (MacKenzie: 2004). There is creativity in science, art and philosophy, even if what is created is different in each domain. We are reminded here of Foucault's idea of the specific intellectual, to the extent that the critique of our systems of knowledge often stems from traversing those systems bringing different discursive rules of how we may think, feel and act into contact with each other to disturb the settled habits of our disciplinary domains.

On the side of practices of resistance, so to speak, we can say that these can now be understood as learning practices. The task of resistance is to learn how to resist and to do this we must be open to the encounters that condition learning so as to create ways of knowing the world that challenge those institutions that we feel stifle our ability to think, feel and act differently in the world. But just as there is no general notion of creativity so there is no general notion of resistance. Resistance is always a particular expression of the potential within an institutional formation. This is why we must talk of practices of resistance. Resistance does not come in readymade forms that can be applied across all domains, all institutions, in the same way. Rather, practices of resistance must be learned from within the systems we hope to resist in ways that will differ depending upon those institutions. The specificity of practices of resistance does not, however, prevent alliances from being constructed across institutional fields. On the contrary, and as we noted above, the fact that any institutional formation operates on a 'grid' or plane of consistency that enables it's movement to connect with others, means that practices of resistance are equally capable of traversing these institutions in ways that can specify the general operation of power at any given time. Just as resistance within an institution needs to be learned, however, so we always need to learn how to move across them in order to form alliances. All of which amounts to saying, to paraphrase Deleuze, that we will never know in advance how people will resist, because they will always learn to do so in ways that are specific to the ways in which they traverse the institutional formations that they seek to challenge. Learning, as the creative process that brings into existence new forms of knowledge about the world and new ways of knowing the world, is not only the 'true condition' of critique, it is the true condition of resistance.

However, this emphasis on creativity, learning, critique and resistance is precisely where those looking for an account of what to do in order to resist and perhaps even to overthrow contemporary forms of domination find Deleuze and Guattari lacking. If we cannot know in advance how people will resist then are we not bereft of clear cut guiding principles that will motivate and justify activism? This problem will be used to set up the next chapter as it provides the backdrop to Alain Badiou's criticisms of Deleuze and the motivation, in part, of his own theorisation of the militant subject of truth. However, for those more sympathetic to Deleuze and Guattari, it is still a problem: consider, for example, the different interpretations of the relationship between structure, event and becoming in the alternative theories of resistance offered by Svirsky (2016) and Sotiropoulos (2013). One of the underlying problems these positions bring to the fore is the relationship between creativity, the creative disciplines and practices of resistance.

Although all disciplines are creative, there is 'a fundamental affinity' between a work of art and resistance. While not every work of art can be said to be a practice of resistance, nor every practice of resistance a work of art, there is 'a certain way' in which art always resists and practices of resistance are art works. How should we untie these knotted claims? Deleuze and Guattari give an ontological definition of art (one that focuses on what it is rather than on how we judge certain objects) when they claim that art brings into being a new bloc of sensations. This is not just a new thing in the world, nor a new way of understanding what we already know, but a new way of experiencing a new world from in-between nature and mind. In this sense, art is fundamentally related to the intensive character of the encounter that engenders thinking within thought and learning within critique. As Deleuze elaborates, he takes this to mean that art resists death – where death is the stifling of all new sensations. This gives us one way of appreciating why art resists 'in a certain way'. It is not that it immediately opposes itself to forms of knowledge and power but in creating new ways of experiencing the world and bringing new forms into the world it resists the tendency of vested interests to constrain the emergence of the new. From the point of view of practices of resistance a similar logic applies. Practices of resistance engender new ways of being in the world, new alliances across institutional domains, which give expression to our desire to live. To live, in this sense, is to be open to new sensations. To the extent that such practices may not be works of art they are captured within that which they are seeking to resist – we might recall that Deleuze refers to this as reformism. If such practices can be understood as works of art it is to the extent that they are able to forge new blocs of sensation in the world. The fundamental affinity between art and resistance, therefore, is the affinity between life and death; resisting death in order to create life, embracing life in order to resist that which is killing us. In 'R is for Resistance', Deleuze puts it succinctly: 'to create is to resist' is a positive statement, one which embraces the fact that people could no longer bear to live in the world if it were not for art. Yes, this is also true of philosophy and science, to the extent that philosophy resists 'stupidity' and science resists 'imbecilic interrogation'. But the affinity between art and resistance is fundamental because it is a matter of life and death.

Is there not a concern, however, that every time we look to specify this link between creativity, critique and resistance we end up reaching for ever greater forms of abstraction? This is true to the extent that we can never know in advance how people will resist, and therefore we can never specify exactly what forms creative practices of resistance will take. The question is one of method: what is to be done in the here and now to critique systems of knowledge and resist institutional power? In other words, the general features of practices of resistance must remain general until they are mobilized in a particular understanding of contemporary institutional forms. We will turn to this task in the last chapter when we look at Deleuze's characterisation of societies of control. The first task, however, is to push the residual concerns about Deleuze and Guattari's aestheticisation of critique and resistance as far as possible; this can be done with the work of their contemporary, Badiou.

# Chapter 4: The Militant Subject
# of a Political Truth

A potential problem with the view of critique and resistance developed in the previous chapters through the work of Foucault, Deleuze and Guattari is that as the philosophical ground is more firmly established so the political edge seems increasingly blunted. As the politics of truth leads us ever more into discussions of creativity we risk losing reference to the idea of truth itself and the motivational force that it has in animating practices of resistance. Although Badiou is not the only thinker to have raised these concerns – there is a lineage to this criticism of poststructuralism that goes back to Taylor (1984) and Habermas (1987) – his work is central to these discussions because he has developed a new event-oriented way of relating subjectivity and truth to politics. Avoiding the temptation of returning to the traditional model of establishing claims about human nature and on that basis articulating the truth about politics, he has formulated an understanding of truth that treats it as the outcome rather than the basis of certain political conditions. It bears some resemblance to the notion of practice led theory, discussed in Chapter Two, but it is accompanied by a systematic rendering of this view that is highly original, deeply compelling and that takes aim at the poststructuralist politics of truth developed up to this point. After a brief reconstruction of his alternative post-foundational account (to use Marchart's term) and a broad outline of his criticisms of Deleuze we will sharpen up what is at stake both in philosophies of the multiple and of the event as well as how these can be used to ground resistance to forms of knowledge and power that uphold contemporary liberal democratic capitalism. In particular, we shall see how Badiou's highly original conception of truth can bring out more clearly what is at stake in earlier considerations of 'the power of truth' (Foucault) and the 'perspectival' truths that emanate from encounters (Deleuze). Ultimately, though, it will be argued that Badiou's appeal to ideas of truth, even if constituted in an entirely novel way, amounts to a return to a dogmatic form of thought that is susceptible to critique. To this extent, it is unable to frame a way of thinking about, or motivate, sustainable practices of resistance to the regimes of truth and power that discipline and control our contemporary lives.

As we embark on the journey into Badiou's radical reconfiguration of truth and its relationship to resistance, it is worth reminding ourselves of the post-foundational nature of his project and why this matters in relation to the poststructuralist politics of truth developed in the preceding chapters. One way to do this is to chart the reception of poststructuralism in general terms. As Foucault's work became recognised as a major innovation in contemporary social and political theory, so it became the subject of much criticism. For the most part, these criticisms charged Foucault with inconsistency. He was presented as a theorist who claimed to do away with transcendental foundations and yet could not avoid them in his work; notably, that it must be true that there is a politics to truth and in this respect there is at least some claim to traditional notions of truth in his work (Taylor: 1984). Habermas (1987) famously referred to these inconsistencies as instances of 'performative contradiction', saying one thing while doing its opposite, and given this it was widely thought, as was the case within many of the feminist responses to his work for example, that his politics of truth could not animate practices of resistance to established hegemonic power (for example, McNay: 1992). There seemed to be a form of 'political quietism' that resulted from this inconsistency vis-à-vis the problem of foundations in his work. Those of a more sympathetic disposition turned to developing an alternative notion of foundation through Foucault's own work (for example, Han: 2002) or that of Deleuze (for example, Patton: 2000); both of which have been strategies deployed in the preceding chapters. On the one hand, it was argued that a more careful, less prejudicial, reading of Foucault's oeuvre could be developed in ways that situated it within rather than opposed to the critical tradition of modern European thought. On the other hand, Deleuze, it was argued, offered a fully-fledged philosophy of difference that could sustain Foucault's politics of truth without privileging identity, human or otherwise. But we have noted how these approaches have led to deeply philosophical considerations of the type that appear far removed from the realities of resistance. There appeared to an impasse: either one was caught on the twin hooks of foundationalism and anti-foundationalism or one veered too close to philosophical abstraction, even mysticism (Hallward: 2006), in defence of an alternative notion of foundation. In both cases a certain political impotency seemed to result. However, an alternative to these approaches was also being developed, one in which Badiou's work has been situated.

Is it possible to think beyond the foundationalism vs anti-foundationalism debate and avoid abstraction and mysticism? For this to be the case, it would seem that philosophical grounds needed to be developed for the *necessarily contingent* nature of foundations. This project took different forms but, as Marchart (2007) has put it, the most compelling of these develop a left-Heideggerian

post-foundational perspective. We noted in the Introduction that his characterisation of post-foundationalism is one that reconstructs Heidegger's notion
of ontological difference (the difference between Being and beings) as political
difference (the difference between the political and politics). The potential of
such approaches is that they seek to think difference and ground at the same
time while also foregrounding the lack of politics in Heidegger's work, and in
poststructuralist philosophies of difference. Although Badiou is suspicious of
political positions that place too much emphasis upon a hypostatised notion of
the political, he can be read as a thinker who presents a particularly sophisticated version of this post-foundational perspective both in terms of his rendering
of the Heideggerian notion of ontological difference and in terms of his understanding of how political events disrupt the everyday world of politics.

Badiou situates his work broadly within Heidegger's claim that knowledge
of the beings that make up the world will never provide knowledge of Being
itself (2005: 1-4). There is, in other words, an unbridgeable divide between what
we know about beings and the question of Being. However, just as Heidegger
thought that this did not rule out the question of Being (we can recall that for
him it was a matter of investigating the ways in which Dasein, our situated-
ness as self-interpreting animals, to use Taylor's phrase, expresses this ontological difference) so to, for Badiou, the question of Being can still be addressed.
Where he radicalises Heidegger is in his rationalist insistence that even if the
nature of Being cannot be addressed through what we know of beings, it can
be addressed in a purely *formal* way through the language of mathematics –
'mathematics is ontology' (2005: 4) – and a variant of set theory in particular.
Moreover, rather than presume that we are situated beings capable of self-inter-
pretation, Badiou focuses on the events that condition us as subjects (here, he
is closer to the later Heidegger rather than the Heidegger of *Being and Time*).
In this sense, though, he is also deeply indebted to event-oriented philosophies
such as that proffered by Deleuze (and, of course, there is a Heideggerian debt
in Deleuze's philosophy; see, Dillet: 2013). However, Badiou's distinct account
of the mathematical language of Being gives a different flavour to his account
of the kinds of event that constitute subjects. In fact, he argues that there are
four types of such event that are expressed in the terms, science, art, love and
politics (Badiou: 2008). Each of these evental types conditions us as subjects
in a manner that enables us to express the truth of our situation, in specific
ways. It is important to note that philosophy is not one of those conditions.
Rather, according to Badiou, philosophy is conditioned by each of these events.
Immediately, therefore, we can notice that Badiou is suspicious of any attempt
to privilege philosophy as the master-discipline, viewing it instead as the discipline that helps us think through whether or not what has happened is really worthy of being called an event that can engender a new subject and a
new truth. We will turn below to the radically new version of the relationship

between philosophy and politics that this creates. For now, it is worth dwelling upon some general features of his theory that brings it into conversation with Deleuze (and Foucault).

Why does Badiou turn to mathematics, and set theory in particular, to address the question of Being? In short, the importance of a set-theoretical account of Being is that it provides a way of articulating multiplicity, albeit a significantly different account to the one we find in Deleuze. As Badiou notes in his book on Deleuze, 'I gradually became aware that, in developing an ontology of the multiple, it was vis-à-vis Deleuze and no one else that I was positioning my endeavour' (2000: 3). Refusing the dialectical impasse imposed on any thought that tries to negotiate the one and the many, Badiou aligned himself to the idea of multiplicity as had Deleuze. However, for all that this signals a deep commonality between their philosophical projects, it also signals a profound difference of approach. We have noted above (chapter 3) that Deleuze substantializes the multiple, and that he often talks about multiplicities in terms drawn from biology. For Badiou, this substantial rather than formal account is signalled by Deleuze's interest in 'the "vital" (or "animal") paradigm of open multiplicities' (2000: 3). Badiou found an alternative way of talking about multiplicities, in 'the mathematized paradigm of sets' (2000: 4). Badiou's philosophy of the multiple is a philosophy of the number rather than the animal. While this may seem, at first glance, like a small difference, in fact it establishes a very profound difference in the relationship between mathematics, science and philosophy. Deleuze's philosophy of multiplicities retains a philosophical privilege, of a certain kind, to the extent that it brings science, biology in large part, under the wings of a philosophy of difference. Badiou's insistence on number distances philosophy from the question of Being, of the multiplicitious nature of Being, by making it a question that can only be addressed in the rigorously formal way that mathematics addresses its most fundamental questions; set-theory. This formalization stands in opposition to Deleuze's substantialization and gives a radically different understanding of the role of philosophy. Philosophy, for Badiou, has no ownership of the question of Being, rather it's task is to think through the consequences of what happens within Being; to think through the implications of the types of event that cut away from Being under the headings, science, art, love and politics. It is the idea that political events condition philosophy that will interest us as we go on. For the moment, though, it is important to recognise that while the difference between animal and number crystallises the opposition between these approaches, Badiou recognises that the task was the same: 'an *immanent* conceptualization of the multiple' (2000: 4). And, in this shared task, we find the importance of Badiou's approach to the discussion of this book: if we have reached the point where an immanent philosophy of the multiple is fundamental to the critically oriented politics of truth in Deleuze (and Foucault) then it may be that we have not dug deeply enough with Deleuze. Perhaps, his substantial account of multiplicities is itself too wedded to a principle of identity and a hierarchical view of philosophy that will render resistance complicit with that which it is trying to resist? Badiou is clear in articulating what he thinks the problem is: Deleuze, the alleged thinker of multiplicity, because he retains the idea that one can identify substantial multiplicities and to this extent restores the privileges of philosophy, cannot but become a thinker of 'the One'. As we were led to ask whether or not Foucault's critique of humanism delved deeply enough into questions of identity in general, we are now led to ask if Deleuze's substantive idea of multiplicity digs deeply enough into the problem of identity to avoid its return.

Badiou constructs this line of questioning through a reading of Deleuze largely based on an extract of the closing line of *Difference and Repetition*: 'A single and same voice for the whole thousand-voiced multiple, a single and same Ocean for all the drops, a single clamour of Being for all beings' (Deleuze: 1994, 304). This is confirmed, however, in his reading of Deleuze's concept of the event: 'And let us also remind those who naively celebrate a Deleuze for whom everything is event, surprise and creation that the multiplicity of "what occurs" is but a misleading surface, because for veritable thought, "Being is the unique event in which all events communicate with one another"' (2000: 11, quoting from Deleuze: 1990, 180). Badiou reads into Deleuze a form of vitalism that draws inspiration from biology in order to give Life to all *organic and nonorganic* forms and occurrences. We can sense the echo of the problem that has animated the discussion so far: in escaping humanism has Deleuze nonetheless fostered a dynamic account of Life that is drawn too heavily from the human construction of biology that Foucault analysed so adroitly? Maybe the animal (or Life in general) comes to replace the human just as the human replaced god, and as such nothing really fundamental changes.

But what are the political consequences of this reading, especially in how we can think about resisting hegemonic regimes of knowledge and power? Badiou has no time for those who think that Deleuze's philosophy of difference, his immanent construction of multiplicities, leads to the liberation of desire in an anarchic manner. Rightly, he calls into question this political elaboration of Deleuze on account of the ways in which it legitimates the return of the sovereign individual, a position completely at odds with Deleuze's insistence on the 'machinic' construction of our sense of ourselves, of will and choice. However, Badiou's sense of the politics at work in Deleuze offers little comfort for those who would want to see in his work the basis for practices of resistance: Deleuze's thought, he says, is 'profoundly aristocratic' because it is profoundly 'ascetic' (2000: 12-13). Drawn away from the rigours of political life by thought, Deleuze is committed to a haughty distance that pronounces on the nature of Life. According to Badiou, for Deleuze 'thinking consists precisely in ascetically attaining that point where the individual is transfixed by the impersonal exteriority that is equally his or her authentic being' (2000: 13). The task of an immanent conception of critique to motivate practices of resistance seems hard to imagine with such ascetic and hierarchical attitudes at work within Deleuze's system.

We can bring these opening remarks to a close with a quote from Peter Hallward: 'philosophy can have no distinctive purpose if thought is not conceived as a creative practice that resists, in its essence, specification by an object, interest or identity' (2003: 28). But what kind of philosophy can resist in this way, and therefore provide the tools with which to resist all forms of knowledge and power that specify the objects, interests and identities that should apparently concern us? Is it Deleuze's immanent critical philosophy or Badiou's account of philosophy conditioned by events? In order to explore this further, it is necessary to outline Badiou's understanding of the ways in which political events condition philosophy.

## Philosophy and Politics

Since the beginning of our investigation into the politics of truth, we have noted that the question of justice is never very far away from our concerns. We saw this in the second half of the discussion between Chomsky and Foucault. It is not surprising as it is generally recognised that the political nature of philosophy was first raised in Plato's treatment of justice in *The Republic*. Western political philosophy, and it is important to note in passing that non-Western traditions of political philosophy do not necessarily give justice this foundational role, seem intrinsically concerned with how to specify and articulate a theory of justice; even if, at times, this question has not always seemed so central. Badiou, for his part, agrees with the standard view: 'From Plato until the present day, there is one word that crystallizes the philosopher's concern in regard to politics: "justice"' (2004: 69). Having set up the relationship between philosophy and politics in this standard way, however, Badiou immediately takes a different step: 'our point of departure must be the following: injustice is clear, justice is obscure' (2004: 69). Although this is a manoeuvre that he is not alone in making (there is an unlikely alliance with Sen: 2009, for example), it is one that strikes a significantly different tone to those who follow Plato in a more standard fashion. The traditional view is that we must articulate a conception of justice in its pure or ideal form in order to see what counts as injustice. Badiou thinks otherwise: 'injustice has an affect: suffering, revolt. Nothing, however, signals justice: it presents itself neither as spectacle nor as sentiment' (2004: 69). Immediately, therefore, we can see that Badiou, for all that he accepts the centrality of the concept of justice, is turning the problem around so as not to privilege a philosophical rendering of the idea before dealing with what animates it in the first place; in this case, the injustices people feel acutely. As he says: 'Justice is a word from philosophy...yet this word of philosophy is under condition. It is under the condition of the political' (2004: 69-70). Rather than have the best minds of the Greek polis contemplate the nature of justice as an ideal form, Badiou reminds us that the philosophical question of justice only emerges because people feel so deeply about the injustices they suffer that they revolt. The precise nature of this suffering and revolt will depend on the political situation. Philosophy's task is to figure out what this suffering and revolt *truly* means, and justice is the name one gives to that truth. In this sense, he says: 'we will term "justice" the name by which philosophy designates the possible truth of a political orientation' (2004: 70).

Of course, we know that 'political orientations' come in many forms. Badiou, perhaps a little summarily, categorises them into two types. First, there are those 'empirical political orientations' that express a 'repulsive mixture of power and opinion'. He has in mind a broad set of these: 'the subjectivity that animates them is that of the tribe and the lobby, of electoral nihilism and the blind confrontation of communities' (2004: 70). In other words, pretty much everything we think of as the to-and-fro of everyday politics. He is quick to dismiss them: 'philosophy has nothing to say about such politics; for philosophy thinks thought alone, whereas these orientations present themselves explicitly as unthinking, as non-thought' (2004: 70). It is important, however, to pause on this statement as it allows us to reconsider the charges laid at the door of Deleuze. Badiou is not averse to asceticism in his own understanding of philosophy; 'philosophy thinks thought alone'. Indeed, Badiou recognised a shared interest in philosophy with Deleuze, an interest in meeting any claims about the 'end of philosophy' with a 'total and positive serenity' and 'active indifference' (2000: 5). That said, it is also clear that his view of the ways in which politics (and science, art and love) conditions philosophy does challenge what appears to be the privilege it finds in Deleuze's philosophy of difference. We can specify what is at stake between them as we turn to the second type of political orientation.

Having dismissed most of everyday political life as irrelevant, Badiou turns to 'those political orientations that have had or will have a connection with a truth, a truth of the collective as such' (2004: 70). Two points are immediately striking: these political orientations 'have had or will have' this feature, such that it is not clear if we can simply attribute this aspect to them without also thinking about how we might attribute it to them in the future. This is not a problem, for Badiou; in fact, it clearly signals his interest in the fact that what constitutes a truth bearing political orientation is something that has to be decided by philosophy, as an on-going process into the future not simply once and for all. The second point to mention is that, despite his dismissive attitude to the tribe and the community he does clearly hold to the idea of the collective.

But what is the truth of the collective 'as such' and why must this truth be established in an on-going philosophical process?

Having cast off most of what counts as political orientations in our everyday world of politics, Badiou unsurprisingly says that those that bear a truth of the collective 'as such' are 'rare' and, in an important conceptual connection to Deleuze, they are 'singularities' (2004: 70). These 'rare' political orientations emerge when the people are engaged in 'nothing but their strict generic humanity' (2004: 70). Only when a political event bursts open the scene of everyday politics in this form can philosophy be truly activated; that is, it is only when such rare, singular and momentous events occur that philosophy is motivated to discern the truth that they bear. This truth is not one of 'destiny' or a 'monumental history' but the singular way in which they express this generic humanity by inducing 'a representation of the capacity of the collective which refers its agents to the strictest equality' (2004: 70). What are these 'rare' political events? It is clear that, for Badiou, they are the great revolutions; those epochal uprisings that have raised the question of what it means to be human, in the strictest sense. Why the qualification, 'in the strictest sense'? This is the case because Badiou wants to distinguish those revolutionary moments that have expressed the interests of some of humanity, for example the bourgeois revolutions that established liberal democracies, from the socialist revolutions that expressed their interests in terms of all of humanity. Having said that, it might seem odd that Badiou puts such a strong emphasis on the idea of equality, given that it animates both bourgeois and socialist revolutions. Once again, though, Badiou's interest in the strict definition of terms comes to the fore. By equality he means 'that a political actor is represented under the sole sign of his or her specifically human capacity' (2004: 71) and not just as an actor that bears a certain interest in their rights of property ownership, for example. He goes on: 'the capacity which is specifically human is that of thought' (2004: 71). However, he understands this capacity in a very original way: 'thought is nothing other than that by which the path of a truth seizes and traverses the human animal' (2004: 71).

This is not a traditional conception of the relationship between thought, subjectivity and truth. Traditionally, we assume that we humans are already thinking animals, animals that already possess the ability to think, and that the task is to think correctly about ourselves, and the world. The more we can align our thought about the world with how the world is, the closer we get to the truth. For Badiou, in contrast, we are animals with the capacity to be 'seized' by a truth that makes us the subjects we can become; in this case, political actors are spurred by their commitment to equality, in the strictest sense. This means that truth comes from outside of us, and it would appear that it emerges in and through those rare political events that carry the truth. Already we can see the general features of this new idea of subjectivity. We can become active agents in the political world to the extent that we are seized by the truth carried by revolutionary moments that, in principle, speak to all. The qualification, 'in principle', is important. Even in the most egalitarian revolutions there will always be those that seek to defend the status quo. Badiou's claim, however, is that such people are motivated by objective interests – in opinion and power, for example – rather than by the pure commitment to becoming a subject that bears the truth, for all. Badiou is clear that it is not easy to bear this truth, and he invokes religious, specifically Christian, terminology in outlining that holding to the truth that has seized us is a matter of fidelity and faithfulness; we become subjects of truth as we remain faithful to the event that has seized us with its truth (Badiou, 2005: 232-9). We shall explore the formal architecture of this idea in more detail in the next section. For now, we should continue with what this means in relation to Badiou's understanding of equality and its relationship to justice.

For Badiou, equality should not be understood as referring to anything objective: 'it is not a question of an equality of status, of income, of function, and even less of the supposedly egalitarian dynamics of contracts and reforms' (2004: 71). To think of equality in these terms is to link it to whatever interests are driving political debate at the time, interests that can only ever express a contingent feature of the social rather than a properly political prescription. As he puts it: 'political equality is not what we want or plan, it is what we declare under fire of the event, here and now, as what is, and not as what should be' (2004: 72). There is an interesting resonance with Foucault's riposte to Chomsky. Whereas Chomsky sought to explain a theory of justice based on human needs and human flourishing, Foucault elicited Spinoza in his account of justice as the name by which struggles are conducted on the battleground of political life. What Badiou adds, and it is a major innovation in political theory, is the idea that we engage in struggles for justice 'under fire of the event'. It is that 'which happens', where this is understood as bearing a generic truth to which all humans can in principle adhere, that conditions our sense of justice in the here and now. Of course, on its own this would remind us of Deleuze's theorisation of the encounters that condition learning and critique. That Badiou takes a different path is indicated by his insistence on the idea that 'once justice is conceived of as an operator of capture for egalitarian political orientations – *true* political orientations – then it defines an effective, axiomatic, and immediate subjective figure' (2004: 72). We have already noted the commitment to truth bearing events, but this additional idea that justice defines an 'axiomatic' subjective figure is worth pausing on. It signals the commitment Badiou has to a mathematized articulation of Being. The axioms of set theory provide the means by which we can account for why it is that some events, those rare political orientations, can be said to bear the truth by which we humans have the capacity to be seized whereas others are mere expressions of historically contingent regimes. As such, 'either the egalitarian axiom is present in political statements or it is not' (2004: 72-3). There is no need to argue about what justice means, ideally, rather we simply have to discern whether or not the political orientation carries the truth within its occurrence. This is the task of philosophy, and why it is always conditioned, in this case, by political events. The usual to-and-fro of political opinions about whether or not this or that arrangement is just, is of no concern to Badiou, even when these seem to animate the most deeply felt practices of resistance, such as the civil rights movements based on different versions of identity politics. Arguing about whether or not this group or that should have access to the world of politics is simply a matter of trading opinions, and redistributing power, without changing anything fundamental about the deeply unequal nature of our political regimes. The task is to analyse the rare and singular irruptions of those who suffer in order to assess whether or not they are resisting in the name of their own interests or in the name of a generic humanity capable of being seized by the truth. Justice is the name that philosophy gives to such rare irruptions when they do appear to all.

Having set up this foray into Badiou's account of philosophy and its conditions as one that was aimed, in part, at dethroning the privilege afforded philosophy by Deleuze, it might seem that we are back to a version of the same privilege. Is philosophy, even if it arrives a little later on the scene of politics, still the ultimate arbiter of what counts as a true political orientation? There is a certain sense in which it is, but we should not underestimate the extent to which it is conditioned by what happens (politically) and that this does at least unsettle that privilege if not entirely remove it. As he says, 'any politics of emancipation...is a thought in act' (2004: 73). And, in this sense, it is clear that Badiou sees a profound link between the activist and the philosopher. He articulates this in terms of justice: 'justice designates the contemporary figure of a political subject' (2004: 75). Although this subject has had several names – the citizen 'in the sense the French Revolution gave to the word', or the 'grass-roots activist' – we live in a time when 'this subject's name must be found' (2004: 75), in part because these, and related designations of a political subject have been compromised by their complicity with liberal democratic regimes. His proposal is that we name this subject, the militant. It is a name that he finds in many sources but perhaps the most influential and we might say surprising place, is in the work of the French poet Mallarmé. Badiou approvingly quotes him: 'let us be militants of restrained action. Let us be, within philosophy, those who eternalise the figure of such action' (2004: 77). In other words, the philosopher and the militant, on Badiou's account are bound together in their respective attempts to understand the truth born within and by those rare political events that seize humanity to think; to think about what it means to be equal in regard to our capacity to be seized by the truth contained within the political event itself.

Whereas Deleuze may have (and it is important to be cautious, as we will have reason to question it at the end of this chapter), given us a picture of the practitioner of resistance as the all-too-philosophical image of the person who learns how to resist, Badiou joins the philosopher and the militant in an axiomatic bond of equality and justice. Driven by a vision of what it means to be a human capable of being seized by the truth contained within these rare events, the philosopher-militant raises the call for equality and justice without having to articulate them as universal norms for social interaction, rather as statements of 'what is, in the here and now' in relation to those who suffer and revolt as a consequence. It certainly seems to be a more radical language, but we must delve more deeply into his system if we are to purge it of lingering doubts that may remain: doubts about why it is that such traditional notions as 'collective', 'equality' and 'justice' remain so central, even if they are reworked in apparently novel ways; doubts about just what it means for a *true* political event to occur on its own terms and in relation to the other types of event he adumbrates (science, love and art – can these not be political?); doubts about his appeal to the idea of the human that we have tried so hard to rinse out of every fibre of the politics of truth.

## Politics as a Truth Procedure

In order to delve more deeply into Badiou's understanding of truth, politics and militant subjectivity we must consider the role of events more thoroughly. We have noted above, that philosophy has a role to play in articulating whether or not a political event contains the seeds of a truly egalitarian conception. In this sense, philosophy is always conditioned by political (and other) events. We can see, therefore, that there is a certain similarity between Badiou's approach and that developed by Deleuze, where the evental encounter conditions the processes of learning that establish a non-dogmatic ground for critique and practices of resistance. And yet, the results that Badiou draws from his philosophy of events appear markedly different from those drawn out by Deleuze. On the one hand, Badiou has little time for the idea of critique; on the other hand, he rehabilitates a more direct political language of equality and militancy that appears, at least, to give a more radical tone to his account of what happens when people engage in resistance. As we have noted since the opening exchange between Chomsky and Foucault, however, we must always be open to interrogating further such apparently radical language if we are to avoid the complicities that can emerge when one expresses practices of resistance in a language that is akin to the language used within those regimes of power and knowledge that oppress and dominate. In this case, we must look more deeply into what Badiou means by a political event.

In the chapter from his book *Metapolitics* that gives this section its title, 'Politics as a Truth Procedure', he deals with this issue directly. It begins with these questions: 'when, and under what conditions, can an event be said to be political? What is the "what happens" insofar as it happens politically?' (2005: 141). These questions neatly formulate the concerns at the heart of our own discussion and, even if we will have reason to question Badiou's own answers to these questions, they encapsulate the problem in a formidably succinct manner. Rather than ask what interests or identities are operative within practices of resistance, or what values they ought to be guided by, the poststructuralist and post-foundational projects share a deep concern with 'what happens' in such practices because this foregrounds an ontology of events that at least promises the possibility of avoiding accounts that hypostatise practices of resistance in explicit or implicit humanist and naturalist frameworks. It is important, therefore, to spend time outlining Badiou's answers to his own questions.

He gives four criteria by which to discern the political nature of an event; that is, by which to discern its capacity to exhibit a political truth. The first of these criteria we have seen already: 'an event is political if its material is collective, or if the event can only be attributed to a collective multiplicity' (2005: 141). In many respects, the key word here is 'only'. Any political event may claim to contain the truth of the situation, the truth of human needs or the truth of the revolutionary transformation of the situation within it. Yet, it is only those that can address 'all' as a 'collective multiplicity' that contain an intrinsic universality that is not simply a function of the address – the idea that we can be addressed by any truth claim, even prejudicial ones – but that is an ontological dimension of the event itself. What this means is that the subject summoned forth by a political event (the citizen, the activist, the militant and so on) must be one that is in principle a subject position *all* can be summoned by in the pursuit of the truth contained within the event. This truth is attributed to a collective multiplicity because it is not a matter of identifying the nature of the subject in advance but of delineating the ways in which a virtual subject position is available to all by way of a procedure that claims that the truth of the event is a truth that all can express. What he calls 'the militants of the procedure' (2005: 142) are those who foster this truth as a 'subjective determination without identity' (2005: 142); that is, they are subjects of the truth of the event without identifying characteristics of the subject to which all such militants must adhere. While the other events that condition philosophy (art, science and love) all have an 'aristocratic' dimension to them, it is only political events that 'declare that the thought that it is, is the thought of all' (2005: 142). This reference to the 'aristocratic' should also remind us of his claim that Deleuze is a profoundly aristocratic thinker because, as Badiou presents him, he valorises an aesthetic, creative, politics of resistance.

We can see this distinction between political and other types of events more clearly if we consider what Badiou calls the 'numericality of the political procedure' (2005: 143). In unpacking this unusual and dense phrase it is important to recall that Badiou presents his investigations into Being through set theory (rather than the vitalism he attributes to Deleuze's animal ontology). Sets are collections of elements that can be numbered. Even more importantly, sets can always be designated as elements of other sets or as containing other sets within them. This insight gives a rich ontology of Being which we cannot go into here (see Hallward, 2003, 'Appendix', for a thorough summary of Badiou's understanding of set theory as ontology), but it does at least hint at why he distinguishes political events from those in science, art and love in terms of numericality. He says: 'the numericality of the political procedure has the infinite as its first term; whereas for love this first term is one; for science the void; and for art a finite number' (2005: 143). The full ramifications of these distinctions are explored in his magnum opus, *Being and Event*. For now, we can say that a true political event is one that has as its first term, the infinite. It is this infinity that determines the true political event as one that can be thought by all and yet thought in a way that does not identify the subjective characteristics of all (because these are infinitely different).

But what does this mean for politics? In Badiou's terminology, the set is always made manifest in a real 'situation'. The situation in this sense always contains the possibility of its infinite expression but it is only when this infinity is expressed in an event we can then say that we have a truly political event. This can be parsed in more recognisable language and Badiou does so in this way: 'only in politics is deliberation about the possible (and hence about the infinity of the situation) constitutive of the process itself' (2005: 143). A true political event, therefore, is one in which all can participate equally in deliberation about what is possible and it is only when this procedure is contained within the event itself that we can say that it contains a procedure that is 'topologically collective' (2005: 142) and that bears a political truth. This is the third feature of events that make them political.

However, it might seem that this does little to express the real conditions of political events to the extent that they emerge against forms of oppressive power. Badiou's fourth criterion of the event makes it clear that this is not the case. Given the potential infinity contained within every situation, why is it that these possibilities are not being constantly explored? His claim, also drawn from his set-theoretical ontology, is that 'every situation has a state' and this idea of the state should be understood ontologically and historically. Ontologically, every situation is named as one, to the extent that the parts and subsets of the situation are codified in certain classifications – this is the set of animals, this is the set of mammals, this is the set of sea-mammals etc. Such statements are, for Badiou, the ontological state of the situation. Historically, the State (which he tends to capitalise when referring to actual political states) tends to name its people through a process of representation; the people are individuals, the people are workers etc. In both cases, the 'state of the situation' designates a higher power – a set of sets – that Badiou reads, historically and empirically, as 'the power of the State' (2005: 144). If, ontologically, 'the power of the state is always superior to that of the situation' then it means that this higher power can never be determined in full or in advance because it can only become visible when its representative power is challenged, in politics, by the presentation of those who resist it: 'empirically, this means that whenever there is a genuinely political event, the State reveals itself...but it also reveals a measure for this usually invisible excess' (2005: 145). Resistance reveals the often-invisible ways in which the State designates people, but in so doing it also creates the means by which this designation can be measured and thus challenged. In this procedure that which is revealed, the higher power of the state and how to resist it, creates the conditions for human freedom. As with equality, however, Badiou has a very particular definition of freedom: 'freedom here consists in putting the State at a distance through the collective establishment of a measure for its excess' (2005: 145). Nonetheless, for all that it is an unusual definition of freedom, we can see that it also contains certain ideas that resonate with 'what happens' in practices of resistance.

Let us draw together some of the themes of this and the previous sections under the idea of what happens when practices of resistance occur, according to Badiou. Motivated by their suffering, people revolt against the situation in which they find themselves. This revolt can take many forms. It can be organised by principles of identity in which people claim that the situation in which they suffer does not respect their sense of who they are as individuals. It can be motivated by power in ways that organise the revolt around questions of access to the dominant regimes of power. Neither of these constitutes a political event, according to Badiou, no matter how deeply people feel about these issues, or how many people mobilise in order to pursue their cause. Such forms of resistance are not really resisting anything because they are utterly complicit in the structures of opinion and power that are already in existence. It is only when a collective multiplicity is mobilised that manifests the idea of a common humanity that one can even begin to think about whether or not such practices are *truly* practices of resistance. It is the task of philosophy to assess the truth claim contained within what happens in and through such practices. At which point, it may be that it can be demonstrated philosophically that the claim to speak for all is in fact merely a disguised version of a sectarian, partial claim on behalf of some. Those practices that speak about flourishing human individuality, for example, may be demonstrably shown to be in league with the operations of capitalism such that they are irretrievably complicit with the hierarchies that capital establishes and thrives upon. In contrast, those practices of resistance that express a common humanity, without identifying the nature of humanity, can be said to constitute a truly political event because they express a properly formal and generic feature of humanity; our capacity to be seized by truth. One of the ways in which this can be discerned is through the capacity contained within our practices of resistance to expose the higher power of the State. This is done by both calling it to account and in the often-violent reactions of the State itself. Part of what is exposed is that the State tends to treat its people as One, as a simply identifiable category that can be moulded and shaped in its interests. Part of the truth contained within practices of resistance is that they have an alternative notion of one expressed within them; that is, they mobilise all without identity in the name of the infinity within the situation. In this sense, they call for a political intervention in which the collective multiplicity that mobilises against the State of the situation remains a collective multiplicity able to express the infinite potential contained within the situation, as a matter of ontological commitment rather than as a value to be shared.

There is no doubt that Badiou has created a compelling account of what happens in practices of resistance based on a formal axiomatic ontology that distances itself as much as possible from all claims of substantive identity, even those embedded within all encompassing notions of Life: but at what cost? One potential cost of his approach is that it is so wary of 'empirical political orientations' that it seems divorced from the most momentous practices of resistance that have defined the modern world. We have already noted his disparaging attitude to the great civil rights movements of the post-WWII period that did much to reshape contemporary liberal democracies. It is equally clear, however, that his strongly formal account gets him into difficulties with some recent events, such as those sometimes referred to as the Arab Spring. His book, *The Rebirth of History*, is an interesting example of this (Badiou, 2012a). Unable to proclaim these events as *true* political events he nonetheless tries to find a way to account for the momentous nature of their occurrence by invoking a series of different types of riot. There is the immediate riot, the latent riot and the historical riot. Only the last of these has any bearing on his category of the political event, but even here it is not exactly clear what is at stake. Historical riots appear to be 'pre-political' in that they bring us to the precipice of an event. And yet, it is by no means obvious how such 'pre-political' occurrences could have this function given his axiomatic account of political events in general. He is forced to waver on just what kind of occurrences these historical riots really are, and it is not at all clear that he manages to justify his claim that they signal the rebirth of history in a way that is consistent with his formal ontology of political events. There is a curious echo of the problem we found in Deleuze: if, for Deleuze, the figure of resistance is the learner, the one who is able to critique what we know from within, then for Badiou the figure of resistance is the militant, the one who is able to hold fast to the truth by which he or she has been seized. In both cases, there is reason to think that the complexities of those who actually resist, such as those who have struggled and continue to struggle for freedom in the Middle East and North Africa, are, in some sense, either reduced to these figures or dismissed. However, in order to dig more deeply into this problem, the problem of how the different figures of resistance conjured up by both Deleuze and Badiou may or may not relate to actual empirical people who resist, we need to examine more closely their respective understandings of the event and how these animate the creation of their respective figures of resistance.

## Events and Subjects that Resist

There are two layers of meaning to the title of this section. First, it refers to the idea that both events and subjects resist the forces of opinion and power that shape the everyday world of politics. Secondly, it refers to the idea that there are events and that then these events condition the subjects that resist such forces. This is a productive doubling of meaning that characterises event-oriented philosophies; in this case, both poststructuralism and post-foundationalism. It is important to recognise that events, in an ontological sense, 'do the work' of resistance if one is to avoid the temptation of basing one's understanding of resistance on ideas of human nature, no matter how thinly construed. For both poststructuralists and post-foundationalists, we will never understand practices of resistance if we do not first and foremost understand 'what happens' in those practices. If we presume that what happens is already shaped by our established notions of the object of resistance or the subjects that resist then we will simply confirm those established notions and implicate practices of resistance in the established regimes of knowledge and power. Thinking about what happens, without presuming such objects or subjects, is fundamental to both positions. And yet, it is equally important that events are *embodied* within subjects if the event-oriented philosophies are to have some critical purchase in the world. As such, every event-oriented philosophy of resistance must also account for the relationship between events and subjects, in particular those figures of resistance such as the specific intellectual, the learner and the militant that we have derived from Foucault, Deleuze and Badiou, respectively.

The problem is that these two necessary elements can be in tension. The subjective embodiment of resistant events may curtail our understanding of the forms of subjectivity that engage in practices of resistance. Put more directly, the people that resist seem to get lost in the philosophical intricacies of event-oriented attempts to avoid their identification. This is a common problem, of course, across all theories that seek to understand forms of resistance. In Marxist accounts, there is a tendency to treat all those who resist as exploited and alienated workers; in liberal accounts there is a tendency to treat those who resist as interested individuals; in both cases empirical examples of resistance complicate these images because those who resist come in many forms, not just as workers or individuals. But this problem has particular bite when one is try- ing so hard to avoid *any* substantive account of the subject that resists. We have come to highlight two differing accounts of the subject that aim to straddle this problem in a productive way: the learner in Deleuze and the militant in Badiou. Both are subjective expressions of event-oriented philosophies, of critique and truth respectively, that hope to capture the necessary embodiment of those that resist in a manner consistent with the respective theories of the event and in a manner that does not deny the ontological multiplicity of subjects; for example, the idea that 'we were always already several' or the idea of a generic humanity. But how do we decide between them? Is there a way of assessing whether or not one or other of these figures of resistant subjectivity is more persuasive? In this section, I will argue that there is, and it all depends on the different ideas of the event animating these positions.

Helpfully, Badiou (2009 [2006]) has articulated the relationship between his and Deleuze's different approaches to the event very clearly in *Logics of Worlds*, in the section 'The Event According to Deleuze' (381-7). In this sec- tion, Badiou draws out four axioms of the Deleuzean event from *Logic of Sense*, which he contrasts with alternatives of his own, so as to 'obtain a pretty good axiomatic for what I call "event"' (2009: 384). The first axiom he discerns in Deleuze's philosophy of the event is this: 'Unlimited-becoming becomes the event itself' (2009: 382). By way of this axiom, Badiou is drawing attention to a feature of Deleuze's philosophy that we have had reason to question above; he is situating the event firmly within Deleuze's allegedly substantive account of vitalism. The fact that Deleuze treats the event as an intensification in the line of Life, the eternal becoming of all forms of existence, means that, the Deleuzean event, according to Badiou, is therefore 'the becoming of becoming'. In contrast, Badiou is committed to a formal account of the event and as such he treats it as a 'pure cut in becoming'. What does he mean by this? In short, it means that, for Badiou, events are moments when the 'inexistent' comes into existence. That which we did not know existed is brought into existence by the event, rather than conceiving of the event as the intensification of that which already exists, even if this is conceived of as Life in general. As such, there is no vital continuity but an excessive eruption from a condition of utter lack. In other words, there is always a void between Being and event, for Badiou, such that the event is that which brings into existence something which is condi- tioned by Being but which has no prior being in itself. The second axiom he uses to distinguish his position from Deleuze's is this: for Deleuze, 'a life is composed of the same single Event, despite all the variety of what happens to it' (2009: 382-3). The unlimited becoming of Life that Badiou detects in Deleuze's philosophy of the event leads him to argue that, for Deleuze, all events are ex- pressions of one big Event; the 'eventum tantum' of *Logic of Sense* (1990: 151).

Here we discern the echo of Badiou's overarching claim that Deleuze, despite ostensible claims to the contrary, is in fact a thinker of the One, in this case the single momentous event that conditions all other events. In contrast, Badiou declares that on his view of events, all events are 'separate' from other events. Declaring that Deleuze's idea of the resonance between events has 'no charm' for him, Badiou characterizes events as the 'dull and utterly unresonant sound' (2009: 385) that brings nothing into harmony. It has to be noted, immediately, that there is something odd about this claim given Badiou's insistence on the same procedure that is contained within different revolutionary events, the procedure by which we are seized by the same generic sense of humanity as beings capable of being so seized. We will come back to this below. The third axiom he presents of Deleuze's theory of the event is this: 'the nature of the event is other than that of the actions and passions of the body. But it results from them' (2009: 383). Badiou is pointing out that for Deleuze events result from bodily interactions but not directly, as this process must take place through the mediator of substantive multiplicities, or bodies without organs; virtual/actual bodies that mediate between ideal virtual events and actual bodies or states of affairs. There are complicated sets of issues at stake here, not the least of which is what is meant by the virtual and the actual in Deleuze's philosophy (see Clisby, 2015, for a recent attempt to unpick different accounts of these terms). The point for Badiou, however, is that this complicated architecture of the event and its relation to bodies ultimately overcomplicates the role of the event in subject formation. In contrast to Deleuze, Badiou claims that it is in the eruption of an event that one can establish a commitment to the truth of the event and, as such, become militant subjects of the procedure. Deleuze, he claims, treats bodies and events as expressions of different orders of being, such that there is an inevitable hierarchy afforded the philosophical treatment of ideal events. Badiou, in contrast, treats embodied subjects as the result of events, albeit a result that has to be continually reaffirmed in the process of maintaining fidelity to the truth contained within the event. The fourth, and last, axiom Badiou assigns to Deleuze's theory of the event is this: 'The event is always what has just happened, what will happen but never what is happening' (2009: 383). According to Badiou, the Deleuzean event resides in the past and it can only be discovered from the perspective of an event in the future that leaves the presence of the event in a situation mysterious. Badiou suggests, for his part, that the event is always 'an atemporal instant which disjoins the previous state of an object (the site) from its subsequent state'. And, therefore, the event 'presents us with the present'. Indeed, it is this last distinction between the different ways that they conceive of the temporality of events that essentially frames their competing event-oriented philosophies.

Badiou is correct, in a certain sense, to say that in broad terms Deleuze treats the event as something that has already happened before the subject becomes aware of what has happened. Similarly, in broad terms, his charac-terisation of his position is correct; for Badiou, the event happens in such a way that the subject then affirms the truth of its happening in a process of fidelity to the event. In previous work, I have referred to this difference as that between a pre-occurrence (Deleuze) and a post-occurrence (Badiou) theory of the event (MacKenzie: 2008). However, simply stating it in these broad terms is insufficient as it merely stabilizes the opposition between them rather than interrogates this opposition in order to garner a more critical understanding of the event and its relation to subjective figures of resistance. We can develop this more critical approach by way of two simple examples.

Considering Deleuze's idea of the event, we can imagine the following situ-ation. We can recall those times when we have walked into a room, for example a room in which a family gathering is taking place, only to sense immediately that something has already happened. There may have been a discussion be-tween family members while we were out of the room about some significant family relationship of which we become aware as walk back into the room; there is a frosty atmosphere and a distinct feeling of awkwardness. In this case, we encounter a new situation and sense that something significant has hap-pened; the event has already occurred. However, in order to know what has happened we have options open to us. On the one hand, we may simply fit this new situation into our established knowledge of the family and dismiss it as something that happens at every gathering. On the other hand, we may seek to learn from within this new situation to see if there really is something new that has occurred. If we follow this latter option then how do we do it? As we noted in the previous chapter, Deleuze's answer is interesting, and neatly captured by Badiou; we must initiate another event in order to discern what has just happened. If this sounds opaque it needn't be as it is often what we do when we introduce humour into such situations. Generally speaking, though, we can know what has just happened if we respond with rhizomatic method or drama-tization. These are, as Badiou correctly states, both future oriented attempts to know what has just happened. Before complicating this picture, though, it is necessary to consider a similar example presented by Badiou.

This example is taken from Badiou's *Being and Event* and it is one of the rare moments in the book when a (relatively) everyday scenario is invoked by way of explanation. He asks us to imagine a knock at the door during a family gathering (2005: 174). When we answer the door we are faced with a person who claims to be a family member that we never knew existed, not even a long-lost brother who we knew about but had no contact with for a long time but someone who claims to be our brother who we never knew existed. In this case, the situation (the manifest family with its set of members) faces an irruptive moment, one in which we are faced with the inexistent. As Badiou explains, at this point the idea of who we are as a family has to be renegotiated and the truth of that event established in ways that will result in a new idea of who counts as a family member. In this sense, Badiou is right to say that his characterisation of the event is about the 'presentation of the present'. That said, it is also clear that the truth of the event can only be maintained after the fact of its occurrence. If the family includes this new member then it will have to remain faithful to this inclusion in family gatherings to come.

While these two examples give us a way of thinking about the pre- and post-occurrence nature of the event in Deleuze and Badiou, respectively, they also suggest a way forward in assessing the relative merits of each. If we assume, for the moment at least, that each of these approaches captures an important feature of the event then is it possible to consider how we might blend them together? For all that Badiou presents the differences between his own and Deleuze's theory of the event in terms of four different axioms, which would suggest that they are utterly incompatible, perhaps there is a way of incorporating them together. There is merit in this approach to the extent that both do seem to express something important about the event – on the one hand, that we often feel it has happened before we are aware of what has happened, while on the other hand we can often only discern if something significant has happened by remaining committed to the idea that it has. If we want to hang on to these intuitions then is it possible to do so from within either Deleuze's or Badiou's characterisation of the event?

We can be clear about one thing: an account that gives room for both of these aspects is impossible within Badiou's formalisation of the event, because he treats the event as a pure cut from the past. It simply does not make sense to say from Badiou's perspective that we can sense that an event has already happened. Badiou's distaste for all substantive empirical accounts of multiplicity means that this reliance upon sense will always be complicit with the objects, interests and identities of the situation, as it exists. However, the link between the two is relatively easy to establish from the Deleuzean side, a point we have noted in the previous chapter as we introduced his conception of the event. According to Deleuze, for all that the event is something that has always already occurred before we are conscious of it happening, it is also something that has to be creatively responded to in the present moment in order that we may learn the difference it has already made. This process of learning can be that of the person who arrives at the door and that of the family already gathered, ideally in a blend of the two as they creatively forge new connections and new ideas of what it means to be a member of this family. In other words, and in contrast to Badiou's summary axioms, there is a dimension of the present in Deleuze's formulation to the extent that we encounter the new in the present and we are the subjects who learn how to express what has happened and what will happen in a process of learning that he, on another occasion, has also referred to as the process of becoming worthy of the event itself (1990: 149). It is, in fact,

Badiou's over-insistence on the idea of the event as cut away from Being that creates the problems: but why exactly? The problem can be crystallised in the difference between a cut as process and a cut that inaugurates a procedure. In Deleuze there is the emergence of the new, there is a sense in which there is a cut from Being, in that something significant is brought into existence that we did not know existed (both the awkward atmosphere in the room and the arrival of the new family member). This cut, however, is itself part of the process of the event; after all, cuts are not instant, they have a processual dimension to them as well. In contrast, Badiou presents the evental cut in such a way that inaugurates a procedure, an already established way of doing something. That which is already established, of course, is the ways in which we respond to being seized by the truth. There is only one way in which this can happen in politics, according to Badiou, because there is only one way that the infinite is expressed. The procedure directs the process, in other words, and in so doing limits the potential of the process to branch out in many different directions, including back and forward in time. As we saw earlier, Badiou treats philosophy as that which eternalises the truth of the event and it is now clear that his insistence on the presentation of the present in the event is in fact an insistence on the eternal nature of the truth it contains, in a thoroughly atemporal fashion. Of course, Badiou recognises this and simply affirms it as part of what must be maintained if we are to maintain the commitment that accompanies subjectivity when it is seized by a true political event. If this commitment is thought to be fundamental then perhaps we align ourselves with this atemporal notion of the event, with the procedure rather than the process, in order to make sense of what happens in practices of resistance?

At stake is the following question: does Deleuze's insistence on the creative response to events diminish the commitment that must accompany resistance? There is no reason to think that it does. While there is no truth of the event that can be established by way of the axioms of set theory or any other formal approach, according to Deleuze, this does not mean that we have to give up on the truths that are created through the process of learning how to think differently. We can recall Badiou's two political orientations: those that are dismissed because they contain nothing but opinion and power, and those that are valorised because they contain the truth. This logic of either/or has no place for the encounters that condition our learning in and with the world and each other that can take us from being unthinking individuals who simply accept the way things are to becoming subjects who resist. Badiou's language of 'being seized by the event' is ultimately a dogmatic obfuscation of a process of learning, dogmatic because it does not get inside the ways in which all truths must be created in and through learning. Learning how to think differently is a process that critiques what we know and critiques the idea that we will only ever know the truth by which we have been seized. But, looking at it from the other side so to speak, learning does not mean that we must give up on our commitment to truth, only that it is better to talk about the truth contained within the learning process rather than a truth that seizes us from outside. For Deleuze, and for Foucault, the politics of truth does not necessarily mean giving up on the idea of truth itself, but rather it means that we invest in the 'power of truth' (Foucault) that is 'always a matter of production' (Deleuze). There are always many truths to discern, these are the subject of commitments that we feel deeply, but they must also be revisable as commitments in the face of new encounters that force us to think differently.

Thinking about the subjective figures of resistance, we can sum up this poststructuralist response to Badiou's version of post-foundationalism like this: the learner can be a militant but the militant will never be a learner. It is this incorporation of the militant within the learner and the corresponding impossibility of the reverse, which establishes the relative power of Deleuze's philosophy of the event against Badiou's. There is a compelling and persuasive aspect to Badiou's idea of the commitment that must follow once the subject is seized by the truth of the event, but it is only compelling to the extent that we are able to understand the moment of being seized by the event from the perspective of the subject that both encounters the new and is able to express the new in their commitments going forward. For all that Badiou has reversed the usual model of the truth such that it is no longer the case of subjects producing truths about the world but truths in the world (of events) producing subjects, it remains dogmatic because he has no way of incorporating the idea that we are subjects capable of learning how to think, act and feel differently; sometimes in radically new ways.

We are now in a position to articulate the event-oriented process in which the subjective figure of the learner as practitioner of resistance can be expressed. When something happens to shake our accepted knowledge of the world and our place in it, we may find that we are driven to understand this new phenomenon, to make sense of this new sensation. If we avoid falling into the dogmatic trap of basing this desire to understand on our will to know then we can engage openly in a process of learning. This process of learning serves as the condition for a critique of that which regimes of power and knowledge think we should know; it is critique as a process of learning how to think, act and feel differently. In order to do this, however, and so as not to reinstate such regimes, we must look to respond creatively by following the rhizomatic connections that this new sensation affords. In so doing, we resist. We resist with the full commitment of remaining faithful to the creative process itself and, in this sense, we become artists of the event bound by our truths but only in the sense that we are bound to know that they are always revisable in light of new encounters. All of which depends on the ways in which regimes of knowledge and power articulate themselves in the face of resistance. Learning, creativity and resistance must always be in the here and now; but what is the here and now that we must resist and how do we make an art of this resistance that is sustainable? It is this question to which we will turn in the final chapter.

# Chapter 5: Resistance in Control Societies

At the end of the last chapter it was concluded that the learner rather than the militant provides the better model of a subjective figure of resistance. It is a better model because it is less tied to the dogmatic claims of truth animating Badiou's account of the relationship between the event and the subject. Rather than being seized by a truth that is rationally discernible within certain rare political events, the learner is able both to make sense of what has happened to forge regimes of knowledge and power that seek to determine our sense of who we are, and to do so by creating alternatives to those hegemonic systems. These two elements constitute a critique and express practices of resistance that are bound together by the open-ended activity of learning about what differences can be made in and through practices of resistance. That this process of learning how to critique and resist is open-ended does not mean that it is without commitment. Indeed, one of the lessons of Badiou's oeuvre is that commitment is vital to sustaining resistance against forms of parliamentary capitalism that will always seek to absorb within itself whatever counter-measures are created. The commitment of the learner, however, in contrast to the commitment of Badiou's militant armed with the truth, is a commitment to the practice of learning itself. In this sense, it is a commitment to the possibilities of new encounters that can challenge the known but it is also a commitment to establishing temporary forms of knowledge that will ground alternative social and political formations, in the here and now. There is, in other words, a commitment contained within learning to which those that resist can adhere: a commitment to the process of creative thinking, feeling and acting expressed in the here and now of resistance. All of which amounts to a defence of the idea of critique and its importance in establishing practices of resistance: without an immanent critique of one's situation there is no hope for sustainable practices of resistance.

But this idea of the relationship between critique and resistance may still seem rather old fashioned. Is there a problem lurking within the seemingly hierarchical position of philosophy over resistance within this idea of their relationship, given its obvious debt to Enlightenment thought? And, from a practical point of view, might it be the case that the historical situation has changed so significantly that this nod to the Enlightenment is simply no longer relevant, given the world in which we live? The previous chapters have addressed the first of these problems in establishing a general idea of immanent critique as a creative practice; an event-oriented critical practice that responds to what has happened to make us the subjects we are by being committed to the process of making things happen differently for ourselves and others. However, this general account of immanent critique repeatedly brings to the fore the need to specify what is happening in the here and now such that we can make a difference. In order to address the latter problem we must ask: what are the dynamics of our current situation such that they can be harnessed in the creation of alternatives to that situation? This is an important question to ask because it reminds us that the critical task of *thinking difference* to its fullest extent must become the creative task of *making a difference* from within the situation in which we find ourselves. In answering it we will see that the figure of the learner must be augmented in a very particular manner; the learner must become the artist, if the idea of difference is to be made manifest as an actual difference in the world. Equally, though, if we are to avoid the modernist tendency to reify certain avant-garde artistic practices, the artist must become the learner in order to create sustainable practices of resistance. This dynamic between learner and artist expresses two ends of the relationship between the encounter with learning that conditions critique and making an actual difference that resists those regimes that claim to know the truth of our nature. The general idea of immanent critique is empty without specification of the resistance that it can engender in the here and now and, in this sense, as much as it is indebted to an Enlightenment notion of critique it also disrupts the universalism of that idea. It is an immanent idea of critique, in other words, precisely because it can only be specified within the regimes of knowledge and power operative at any given moment, and there is an art to those practices of resistance. However, a claim such as this is best demonstrated rather than simply stated.

In this chapter, therefore, I will reconstruct Deleuze's (1995) account of the shift from disciplinary societies to societies of control in order to address what is required of critique and resistance, today. This will provide insight into the ways in which critique can be animated, or perhaps more accurately re-animated, in our contemporary situation such that it will foster resistance. Moreover, we will turn to the thorny question of the truth contained within the arts of resistance in order to show that creative practices contain the commitments necessary to inform resistant acts that will enable the transformation of those regimes of knowledge and power that make us think that there is no alternative. The truth to which the learner as practitioner of resistance adheres is that there are always alternatives (because the learner is the thinker of pure difference), even if the evaluation of these is a matter of pragmatic experimentation found within a certain account of artistic practice (because the artist is the one who makes a difference). As we will see, the learner becomes the artist as critique becomes resistance, and the artist becomes the learner as resistance becomes critique. This relation of mutuality is key to understanding how we can resist the apparatuses of control that increasingly dominate our lives in contemporary liberal democracies. As such, just as we can say that without an immanent critique of control societies there can be no sustainable practices of resistance, we can equally say that without practices of resistance there is no hope for a critique of our current situation.

## Critique in a Time of Control

It is by no means obvious that critique has a role in our contemporary world. If our contemporary situation has changed markedly since the time of Kant then it may be that we need to give up on the very idea of critique as a source of understanding what we should resist and how we should resist it. In this section, however, it will be argued that although we do now live in changed times, the idea of critique still has radical purchase. That we may need to reformulate what we understand by critique is not a problem; such reformulations are the bread and butter of post-Kantian thought. That these attempts to reformulate critique have not become exhausted is the issue, as it is clearly the case that many in the current philosophical scene think that it has reached a state of exhaustion (most notably, Latour: 2004). In order to see more clearly what is at stake, however, we must follow Deleuze's account of how post-disciplinary societies function. In other words, we need to reconstruct the brief but illuminating account in his 'Postscript on Societies of Control'

Deleuze's essay is split into three sections: 'History', 'Logic', and 'Program', with the middle section afforded the most space. In the 'History' section, Deleuze gives one of the most succinct and yet instructive accounts available of how Foucault understood the emergence of disciplinary societies; how, once established, disciplinary institutions function; and, how they were already fading out of existence in the aftermath of the Second World War. According to Deleuze, Foucault's analysis of the 18$^{th}$ and 19$^{th}$ centuries led him to trace the emergence of disciplinary societies that 'succeeded sovereign societies', a relatively short-lived moment that reached its 'apogee at the beginning of the 20$^{th}$ century' (1995: 177). While Deleuze stresses that the transition from sovereign to disciplinary societies 'took place gradually', notably in contrast to those readers of Foucault that over-emphasize discontinuity as an interpretive frame for his genealogical investigations (for example, Badiou, 2012b), it was clear by the beginning of the twentieth century that there had been a 'transformation from one kind of society to another' (Deleuze, 1995: 178). 'Major sites of confinement' that operate by segmenting individual lives and populations into designated roles and functions characterize this new disciplinary model of society. This segmentation is most obvious as one moves from one site to another: 'you're not at home, you know', 'you're not at school, you know' (Deleuze, 1995: 177). But, as Deleuze acknowledges, Foucault – the great analyst of disciplinary societies – already knew, as he was writing *Discipline and Punish*, that disciplinary institutions were breaking down and new forms of (biopolitical) governance were taking hold. Deleuze adapts an idea from William Burroughs when he labels the emergent post-disciplinary apparatuses, forms of control (Deleuze, 1995: 178).

The section titled 'Logic' has three component parts; it deals first with the nature of institutions and their relation to each other within societies of control; it then moves on to a discussion of how this affects individuals at the personal and collective levels; before ending with a discussion of the machines that correspond to control (all the while sharpening the contrast between discipline and control). It is worth taking each element in turn. Where disciplinary institutions were characterized by 'independent variables', control societies operate by way of 'inseparable variations' (Deleuze, 1995: 178). In a justly famous distinction, he argues that disciplinary confinement *moulded* individuals according to roles and functions whereas controls are defined by *modulations* that traverse both the social field and the life-course of individuals. He gives two main examples; the shift from factories to businesses and the shift from schools as sites of discipline to the idea of continuing education as a mode of control. It is worth quoting what he says about the latter:

Even the state education system has been looking at the principle of 'getting paid for results'; in fact, just as businesses are replacing factories, school is being replaced by continuing education and exams by continuous assessment. It is the surest way of turning education into a business (1995: 179).

On the one hand, we can say that this is a prescient remark borne out by the recent history of state education at all levels. On the other hand, we might say that Deleuze didn't entirely foresee that the same logic was beginning to turn businesses, and other institutions, into education systems.

Turning to the forms of political subjectivity engendered by control, Deleuze contrasts the processes of *individuation* operative within disciplinary institutions with those processes of *dividuation* that signal control. 'We are no longer dealing with a duality of mass and individual' he says, rather 'individuals become dividuals and masses become samples, data, markets or banks' (Deleuze, 1995: 180). What is a dividual? A dividual is a bundle of elements held together in variation rather than in reference to a unitary subject. Where disciplinary institutions segmented the life-course of individuals into separate subjective roles and functions, control modulates elements of subjectivity across the entire social field. Where disciplinary societies required institutions to normalize behaviour in subject positions, control societies maximise dividuated behaviours without norm.

How are such processes of dividuation made operative as control? Deleuze turns to the machines that correspond to this form of society – information technologies and computers – adding that 'this technological development is deeply rooted in a mutation of capitalism' (1995: 180) from proprietorial forms of production to metaproduction such that 'marketing is now the instrument of social control and produces the arrogant breed who are our masters' (1995: 181). Although Deleuze is clear that this correspondence should not be taken to indicate any hint of a technological determinist reading of the base-superstructure relation (1995: 180), it is clear that this section places an emphasis upon technological forms through which control functions, a feature that is then further cemented in the last section.

The last section, 'Program', has a dual function that plays on two senses of the word. It begins with a summary remark regarding the ways in which contemporary societies embed programmable mechanisms of control within information and computational technologies (such that, Guattari's imagined city of passwords is becoming a reality). But it also contains the seeds of a (political or revolutionary) program to challenge control. In relation to the former, Deleuze returns to the brief examples of how disciplinary institutions are breaking down and being supplanted by mechanisms of control located in the continual modulation of dividuated subjects. In relation to the latter, he says that we must find both 'the basic sociotechnological principles of control mechanisms as their age dawns' (1995: 182) and in so doing see if we can glimpse the outlines of future forms of resistance to control.

However, if we are to fill in the sketch of resistance he offers at the end of this essay along the lines outlined in this book, then we must first ask: what is the status of critique in control societies? The question is framed in this way because it is not clear what, if any, role critical theory, broadly understood, can play in control societies. It is a problem that Antoinette Rouvroy has expressed very clearly (although she refers to the role of critique after the 'computational turn'):

I wonder if it is still possible to practice critical thinking after a computational turn, which despite its pretences to 'objectivity', appears as a turning point away from the ambitions of modern rationality anchored in empirical experiment and deductive – causal – logic and, despite its promises of personalization and better taking into consideration of individual merits, needs, abilities, preferences, does not address individuals through their reflexive capabilities or through their inscription within collective structures, but merely through their 'profiles' (2012: 144).

Moreover, she argues that there are three key features of life under the 'computational turn' that make critique difficult to practice. First, the background of 'real life' (no matter how constructed we might think this is) is becoming 'indistinct' (2012: 144). Secondly, the modern framework of judicial and scientific testing through experiment has been superseded by 'the real time, pre-emptive production of algorithmic reality' (2012: 144). Thirdly, what she calls 'algorithmic governmentality' is a regulative form without subject, such that it does not allow for or enable the reflexivity necessary for critique (2012: 144). This is a delimitation of the problem of critique today with which it is hard to disagree: it is no longer possible to rely upon the reflexive capacities of subjects, especially if these are deemed to be part of our innate cognitive apparatus, in order to ground critique in societies of control. However, a broader framing of this problem can be provided that in turn will slightly alter her account of the status of critique today: Rouvroy's account of the potential that remains within transgressive forms of critique is less convincing than her diagnosis of the problem because her solution remains tied to disciplinary regimes, when we are in fact in a post-disciplinary context of control.

From the perspective of current theoretical debates, we can see that it is indeed the case that there is an increasing consensus that the age of critique has come to an end. Certainly, it remains the case that the idea of critique as a practice of establishing the limits of knowledge available to a reflexive subject that emerged within sovereign societies is still an important strand of those inheritors of Kant committed to the communicative turn (notably, second generation Critical Theory, hermeneutics and varieties of second wave feminism). Moreover, for those suspicious of the exclusionary and disciplinary consequences of such critical practices, it is still important to reframe the idea of critique as a practice that transgresses those subjective limits by exposing their historical and cultural contingency (notably, third-wave feminism, post-Marxism and certain strands of poststructuralism). Critique as a practice of stepping beyond the limits of possible knowledge, for some, came to replace the idea that critique should establish the limits of legitimate knowledge. However, if it is the case that we live under regimes of 'algorithmic governmentality' or, what we would call, an emergent post-disciplinary society of control then it is by no means clear what, if any, new practice of critique is appropriate for this new epoch. In the face of this uncertainty, it is perhaps not surprising to note that the apparently radical cutting-edge of contemporary philosophical inquiry has sought to leave behind the idea of philosophical and practical critique altogether. It has become increasingly commonplace to argue that critique is either exhausted such that it should be replaced by a deeper appreciation of matters of concern (Latour, 2004; Harman, 2011) or, that the tendency of parliamentary-capitalism to recuperate critical positions means that it should be replaced by a revitalized politics of commitment (Badiou and Žižek, 2009). However, in line with

Rouvroy, I take it that the status of critique in control societies can be positively reframed and that it is necessary to do so if we are to ward off the dangers of a conservative embrace of that which simply concerns us most, or a dogmatic position of commitment in the name of a subject of truth that can simply break open and away from the democratic marshalling of fixed and unchallenged opinions. In this sense, critique has a history. It has a history, not in the sense that it must mobilize historical material to ward off a-historical tendencies, in the manner of historical materialism or genealogy for example, but rather in the sense that the very idea and practice of critique must adapt as each new social formation appears. But what remains of critique if there is no recourse to the reflexive subject, its communicative variant or the transgression of limits set by both? And what role might it have if we are to find a path between concern and commitment?

In order to answer these questions we must delimit further the logic immanent to control such that we can engender a critique of it and resistance to it. In order to do this we probe this logic further than Deleuze, now that the logic is more apparent to us, and ask: what is an algorithm? An algorithm is a self-contained step-by-step set of operations to be performed. There are three key elements to this definition that are important for our discussion. First, while a human may perform the algorithmic task, increasingly it is a task that is outsourced to computers. Rouvroy puts it succinctly when she says that algorithmically produced knowledge is no longer produced by humans *about* the world, rather it is 'produced *from* the digital world' (2012: 146). Secondly, an algorithm is a process, but importantly it is a finite and contained process. In this sense, it is correct to talk of algorithms as 'IF...THEN...functions', where IF specifies the conditions of the operations and THEN specifies the consequences of the operation. Thirdly, that which is operated upon can be referred to as data, information, code and so on but the most useful approach is to follow Lazzarato's (2014) treatment of these as *signs*. The sign can in principle take any 'computable' form: it may be a number, but it could just as legitimately be a visual symbol, a bodily gesture, a click on a keyboard, a smell; even a user's attentiveness or not to parts of a screen (Bueno, 2017). In sum, therefore, the initial definition of an algorithm can be parsed as follows: an algorithm is a finite process of establishing consequences from conditions by virtue of operations that act upon signs. When understood in this way, and to the extent that Rouvroy is correct in saying that such algorithms govern us, then it is clear that control societies present a fundamental challenge to the idea of critique.

In the context of the present discussion, there are three points that can be made to outline a new idea of critique that can meet the challenge of control societies. The first is a small additional point to the conclusion of the last chapter: Badiou's emphasis on formal procedures over and above processes plays directly into the machinations of algorithmic governmentality. In this sense, it is important to turn the tables on the criticisms he and others make of Deleuze and Deleuzian inspired politics. While it is sometimes claimed that a Deleuzean politics of rhizomatic connectivity is the hand-maiden to neo-liberal forms of capitalism (Boltanski and Chiapello, 1999), it is important to counter this argument with the distinction between procedures and processes. The problem with Badiou's idea of politics as a truth procedure is precisely that it follows the algorithmic structure of 'IF...THEN...'. If the political event is of a certain form then it will contain a truth that will seize subjects and if they are so seized then they must remain faithful to that by becoming a militant subject of the initial political event. It is Badiou, not Deleuze, who has inadvertently adopted the algorithmic model as the model of resistance and to this extent risks its easy recuperation within the very structures of knowledge and power that he is seeking to resist. In short, in pitting his theory against an outmoded conception of deliberative democracy, he has not hit the right target and, inadvertently, adopted the formal qualities of the new system of dividuated democratic control. Secondly, we can understand why it is that Badiou and others have called Deleuze and Deleuzeans to account for their complicity with contemporary capitalism in that the emphasis on rhizomatic connectivity seems to provide a quasi-ideological defence of contemporary systems of control. However, recalling that an algorithm is a *finite* process of establishing consequences from conditions by virtue of operations that act upon signs we can see the difference that establishes rhizomatics as an immanent critique of algorithmic systems. Rhizomatics is a method for forming, in principle, infinite connections between signs that does not produce pre-defined results. In this sense, algorithms are finite processes – procedures – whereas rhizomatics is a way of connecting the signs in an infinite number of ways. As such, rhizomatics is a process-oriented method of connection that critiques algorithmic procedures from within; immanently. Nonetheless, and this is the third point, it is important to specify how rhizomatics functions as a critique of control systems. As we noted in Chapter Three, it is never enough to say that rhizomes exist and therefore radical connectivity simply happens. The multiple, we must always remember, must be made, and it is made by actively initiating the two-sided process of subtracting the unique and the One from all collectivities (including the collectivity that is the 'self'). By subtracting the unique individual from the group we can then map the ways in which this individual may engender connections across the whole plane of consistency, now defined as the plane that enables the functioning of control. The point here is that the unique individual has the potential to be connected across algorithmic systems that have a relative autonomy thereby disrupting their functioning by initiating new and unexpected connections. On its own, however, this might simply encourage the growth of algorithmic functions rather than stifle them. It is for this reason that there must also be the rhizomatic process of resisting the re-establishment of the One. In this instance, this means creating connections that are not amenable to the defined end of algorithmic systems. As both Deleuze and Badiou, in their different ways, recognise, this means constructing multiplicities that are in principle open ended by virtue of the ways in which they engender further connectivity without a subject position to anchor them. Where Badiou ultimately circumscribes this in the name of a formal conception of truth, Deleuze and Guattari do not by virtue of the ways in which they conceive of the creative potential present within substantive encounters that condition learning and critique. But what does this mean in terms of enacting forms of resistance within control societies. In order to push in the direction of resistance it is important to elucidate the relationship between the learner able to critique control and the artist able to resist control.

## Resistance in a Time of Control

The problem of critique in control societies is also a problem of how to resist; how to enact critique as a challenge to hegemonic systems of domination and oppression. As noted at the end of the previous section this is a two-sided rhizomatic task: it is both the de- and re- territorialisation of established systems to forge new connections between unique individuals and signs, and it is also the task of forging new collective assemblages across these newly established terrains. In the discussion thus far, the subjective figure of such resistance has been the learner, rather than Badiou's militant, but it has also been noted that this prioritises the problem of critique rather than resistance. In thinking about how to make manifest forms of resistance that embody this dual task of rhizomatics as a practice of resistance it is useful to consider the relationship between the learner and those that make a difference as well as those that can think difference to its fullest extent. The subjective figure that resides on the 'making' side of resistance is the artist. In elaborating upon this claim it is important to establish what is at stake: the artist and the learner are two ends of the relationship between critique and resistance; while the learner is the figure that grounds the critique that animates resistance, the artist is the figure who makes critique manifest as resistance. They are intimately connected expressions of the process-oriented understanding of the relationship between critique and resistance. In other words, they are the figures that express the art of the event that establish the profound linkage between creative practices and resistant acts.

In *Chaosmosis*, Guattari turns to art and aesthetics to understand how we might challenge the emergent forms of control that shape contemporary liberal capitalist democracies. He notes that 'artistic cartographies have always been an essential element of the framework of every society' (1995: 130). Although, artistic production has become specialised under contemporary capitalism, it retains its function as 'a vital element in the crystallisation of individual and collective subjectivities' (1995: 130). This phrase has important resonances with the themes developed earlier in this book. We can see the appeal to the vital force of art as one that resonates with Deleuze's long-standing interest in vitalist philosophy. Equally, we can note that it is never simply an appeal to a mystical force of Life that will suffice; this vital element is only interesting to the extent that it explains how 'individual and collective subjectivities' can be constructed beyond those that are assumed to be natural, given, universal and fixed. As he goes on, 'the work of art, for those who use it, is an activity of unframing, of rupturing sense, of baroque proliferation or extreme impoverishment, which leads to a recreation and a reinvention of the subject itself' (1995: 131). The crucial elements of this definition are to be found in the qualifiers 'for those who use it' and 'is an activity' as both of these establish that art, for Guattari has a function and only if it is guided by this function will it provide a challenge to the world in which it is made. The function is described in terms of the event; art is an event to be encountered and it is only when it is treated as such that it can escape the logic of consumption and 'generate fields "far from the equilibria" of everyday life' (1995: 131). Less concerned with art movements and classifications, Guattari treats art as that which is able to develop 'a mutant production of enunciation'; simply, an echo of the idea that there is always more to be said than we think. Where this idea of art is especially important, though, is in the way that Guattari always links artistic activity to both a process of creative singularisation and a process of social mutation.

In the production of art, we find both the de- and re- territorialisation of semiotic space (how we think, act and feel can be transformed) and the singular expression of a new collective assemblage that can mobilise new ways of thinking, acting and feeling between subjects. In other words, the two-sided nature of rhizomatics is expressed in the very process of artistic production: there is both a challenge to the One and the creation of something unique. However, it would a mistake is to think that the challenge is only 'artistic' in the traditional sense and that the 'unique' is the art object. The figure of the artist must not be fetishised, rather it is the activity of producing events which rupture dominant systems of signs that is foregrounded and while this is often done by those we traditionally call artists it is equally clear that for Guattari those who we don't think of as artists but who do engage in such processes are engaging in art. As he says: 'this is not about making artists the new heroes of the revolution, the new levers of History! Art is not just the activity of established artists but of a whole subjective creativity which traverses the generations and oppressed peoples, ghettoes, minorities...I simply want to stress that the aesthetic paradigm – the creation and composition of mutant percepts and affects – has become the paradigm for every possible form of liberation' (1995: 91). Similarly, that which is produced is not simply an art object as it is the construction of a singularity; even when it is recognisable as a traditional art object, it only functions as art, on this definition, because it creates the potential for the formation of new forms of individual and collective subjectivities. What links both is the idea of the artistic practice as a process that takes us from rupture to creation (and back again); in just the same way that learning is a process that takes us from the encounter with the unknown to the known (and back again).

We can see how this relates to control societies when we consider the figure of the artist more closely. Genosko has given a neat summary of Guattari's view of subjectivity in general: 'the Guattarian subject is an entangled assemblage of many components...the individual is like a transit station for changes, cross-ings and switches' (2008, 106). This view of the subject is one that expresses the complex ways in which the algorithmic functions through our sense of self to make us who we are in control societies. But it also contains the idea that we are able to change the ways in which the algorithms function, to the extent that we are 'the transit stations for changes, crossings and switches'. The figure who is not simply constructed through the apparatuses of control but able to change the direction of the algorithmic function is the artist. Or, as Anna Cut-ler has put it, this figure is the artist-as-process: 'the artist-as-process has ways of operating that identify dominant transmissions and in the acts of creativity... of imagining, of generating a new idea, of creating and making a difference, disrupting the forces of mass-transmission' (2013, 356). In this discussion, the formulation of the artist-as-process is particularly helpful. The very conditions of control that shape our contemporary forms of governmentality are also those that enable immanent forms of resistance to control, because there is always the potential to switch around the direction of the 'IF...THEN...' functions in order to forge new connections. Even more importantly, though, there is always the potential to stall and disrupt these functions in the name of a 'what if'; the process of singularisation that accompanies the disruption of the algorithms themselves. In this we can see an echo of Deleuze and Guattari's idea of art as that which approaches the infinite through the construction of the finite. The importance of expressing it in these terms is that it also connects us back to the learner. The learner is the figure that approaches the infinite as infinite – the idea of pure difference that destabilises all claims to identity – whereas the art-ist makes a singular and finite difference that manifests pure difference in the world, so to speak. The artist acts in order to think, the learner thinks in order to act; both express the eventual qualities of critique and resistance respectively.

What is the art of resistance, today? It is the ability to disrupt the algorith-mic flow of contemporary governmentality by connecting signs that don't func-tion algorithmically; that is, subtracting the unique in the algorithm in order to form collective assemblages of 'what if' rather than 'IF...THEN...'. The site of disruption is found in the encounter and it is the task of the learner to critique control from within that encounter by animating it as an artistic practice: the learner becoming artist. As artist the creative expressions of that activity of critique is found in the mobilisation of a people yet to come: the artist becoming learner. In between the two, there are creative practice and resistant acts on both sides: but what, if anything, remains of truth?

## The Politics of Truth in a Time of Control

The previous two sections of this chapter have established that there is still a role for critique within societies of control and practices of resistance that can disrupt the seemingly all-encompassing algorithmic flow that characterises our current condition, within contemporary liberal democracies. That said, it is clear that both critique and resistance must be rethought if they are to have this role. Critique can no longer be conditioned by the reflexive subject able to determine the proper limits of the known, nor the transgressive subject able to go beyond the limits of the disciplines that establish what is known. Rather, critique must embrace the processes implicit in algorithmic governmentality so as to expose the finite nature of their essentially procedural functioning. This image of critique requires opening up the possibilities intrinsic to encounters with the unknown; the possibilities of learning how to connect the singular to the singular in order to form collective assemblages of mutant enunciation (and mutant thought, vision, feeling and action). Such mutant forms, however, need to become actual forms and not merely the preserve of the thinker of pure difference. In this sense, the critic as learner must also become what Cutler (2013) calls the artist-as-process, a figure of resistance to the dominant systems of knowledge and power capable of expressing the infinite capacity of processes to connect anything with anything in new ways of speaking, thinking, seeing, feeling, and acting. The artist, in this sense, is the one who can bring us to the infinite connectibility of process by way of finite creations of individuality and collectivity. The learner and the artist, therefore, are two sides of the relationship between critique and resistance, blended together in the activities of thinking and making a difference in a world that fundamentally blocks thinking and making. This is especially true within control societies which apparently embrace the smooth flow of connectibility and difference but that actually only do so in the name of more insidious forms of control over our individuality and collective existence.

But raising the idea of truth again in this context is not obvious, not least because we have travelled so far in our critique of the idea of the truth of politics in search of the politics of truth. One way of expressing the importance of Badiou's intervention, however, is that he provides a genuinely novel account of the nature of truth that can help us grasp what has been at stake in the enigmatic remarks about 'the power of truth' and the 'truth which we deserve' we have encountered in the work of Foucault and Deleuze, respectively. Truth is a matter of commitment, not of designation, coherence or consensus. Nonetheless,

Badiou's idea of the truth to which we should be committed remains too dog-matic because it is tied to a purely formal procedure emanating from rare polit-ical events. Embracing the potential within all events, all those encounters that engender new forms of what matters or what is significant, allows us to think of this commitment as the commitment of the learner to the process of learning itself and the commitment of the artist to the process of making a difference. Can we dig more deeply, though, into the status of this commitment to truth within contemporary societies of control? In particular, is it possible to hang on to the idea of the truth of art in a world governed by algorithms in the name of control? These are questions that have been addressed by Boris Groys in his article, 'The Truth of Art' (2016).

Groys begins his essay in typically direct form: 'the central question to asked about art is this one: is art capable of being a medium of truth'. This is the central question, he argues, because if it is not then art can only be thought to be a matter of taste and design; art dissolves into a decorative craft. Unless it has the capacity to serve as 'medium of truth' it will not have any independent power. Groys sets the scene for his discussion by suggesting that the power of art is often thought to be simply the product of individual artists who are able to find ways of taking personal responsibility for the expression of ideas in a world dominated by 'big collectivities: states, political parties, corporations, scientific communities and so forth' (2016: 1). Only art, it is sometimes thought, can en-able the individual to find a form of expression that is not already dominated by the political and disciplinary objectives of such 'big collectivities'. Something of the authentic remains in our common sense understandings of the artist and artworks; by bringing into existence new forms of sensibility the artist is able to challenge the interests of power and money with a view to influencing the world around us. He argues that there are two ways in which such influence has typically been formulated. First, the artist is the one who can 'send a mes-sage' to the world through their work. Tracing the lineage of this idea through the ancient and Christian traditions of art up to the political art of the early twentieth century, Groys argues that this function of art requires a common language between artist and audience within which the artist can evoke the authentic. It was an idea of shared language and values that came under attack by the modernist avant-garde who sought to produce work that was actively disliked by the public, a form of counter-message to the shared assumptions of religious and political 'big collectivities'. As such, with the avant-garde we see the emergence of a different way of understanding the truth of art: we move from the production of message to the production of things. In this mode, the truth of art does not depend upon a common language but on a common set of technologies. The aim was to intervene at the level of these technologies so as to create 'new environments' at the material, rather than the ideological, level. Whatever truth there was in the historical avant-gardes it was a truth linked to utopia, the idea that there are new and better possible worlds that can be made from the material of this broken world. But just as the production of messages was reincorporated into the ideological frames of the 'big collectivities' so too the technological innovations of the avant-garde were reincorporated into the conservative tendencies of contemporary institutions; most notably, of course, the museum.

Groys' survey of these issues begins to touch on the question of control as he turns to what has happened 'in recent years': 'the internet has replaced traditional art institutions as the main platform for the production and distribution of art...the internet is the place of production and exposure of art at the same time' (2016: 6). He has an intriguingly broad image of what this means. For Groys, it is not just that the internet is increasingly a medium of artistic practice, it is also the storehouse of artworks, the site in which the artist creates their public profile, the place where the art of the artist is intimately connected to the life of the artist (working on one's CV while ordering groceries on-line), all of which blurs the line between the artwork and the documentation of the art and the artist through the medium of the internet. While there is still privilege given to the real object, its documentation (and all that goes with it) has become as legitimate as the work itself. In some sense, therefore, 'the actual work of the contemporary artist is his of her cv' (2016: 7). As Groys argues, though, this changes the nature of the relationship between the artist and his or her public. The person who sees art, for example, is no longer present. But even more than this, they are not even present behind a computer screen. The spectator of contemporary art 'is the algorithm' (2016: 8).

What does this mean in relation to the truth of art? According to Groys, it is no longer possible to conceive of the artist as the authentic producer of messages or of things because both of these notions presumed that the artist had a certain 'surplus of vision' where the artist could see beyond the horizons of contemporary publics in order to enable them to say and to see what they simply could not. Today, however, 'under the conditions of the internet the surplus vision is on the side of the algorithmic gaze' (2016: 8). Perhaps, Groys ponders, 'artists can still see more than the public but they see less than the algorithm' (2016: 8). He sees this as having an interesting consequence. Where once the artist was extraordinary, a messenger or a visionary, now the artist is the paradigm of how we all create and document our lives on the internet: we have entered an age of the mass production of art. And, 'today there is nobody who is not involved in artistic activity of some kind' (2016: 9). The paradigmatic nature of the artist, in these conditions, is that he or she is able to express the non-identity of all of us in an age of the internet and algorithmic control. Although the artist genius has been reified at least since the modern age, the artist is now the one who is able to disappear most effectively into the documentation of their work, into their life on the internet and into algorithms themselves. The truth bearing capacity of art today is that it can say to us all 'I am not what you think I am' (2016: 9). For Groys, this means that the museum is no longer the place for the effective archiving of artworks and artists. In the context of this discussion, it has broader consequences.

Recalling Cutler's (2013) idea of the artist-as-process we can turn Groys's negative ending into a more positive critique and practice of resistance. While he claims that the artist is disappearing into the algorithm, so the artist-as-process can find the infinite connectibility within it to emerge as a new mutant form. The process will always exceed the procedure, as argued above in relation to Badiou, and in this way it provides the means to critique the limited, finite logic of algorithmic governmentality and the resources from which to draw for new forms of engagement and experimentation in a world of infinite connections. The artist-as-process is the creative learner who has first and foremost committed to learning how to become a learner. As artist, however, this commitment is established and framed by the on-going pursuit of practices that mutate the given world that we think we know so well. This process embodies the rhizome constituting operation of n-1: subtract the binding identity and locate the singular. As Cutler puts it, in Guattarian language: 'It is therefore the interruption through re-singularisation that will both inform and be informed by the creation of new social practices...As such, one might consider not just the subject to be an artist, but social practice as artist' (2013: 357). And in this re-singularisation of habituated knowledge, the experimental attitude that brings the artist-as-process into subjective form and/as social practice we can find the optimistic response to Groys's otherwise perceptive analysis. Indeed, we can sum up this optimism by adding to Deleuze's insistence that 'to create is to resist'. We can now say that it is better to say that 'to create is to resist is to create' and so on, in a process oriented immanent critique of algorithmic truths and a practice oriented construction of new truths whose power resides in the infinite connectibility they express. There is a truth to art, today; it resides in it's power of turning 'I am not what you think I am' into 'I am what I am becoming, whatever you think I am'. Learning to resist, today, involves experiments in becoming more connected than the algorithms allow, and in the process creating expressions of what we can become, despite whatever the algorithmic functions of high finance and social media think they know about us, individually and collectively. The learner as critic and artist-as-process join in a mutual combat against the algorithmic procedures that claim to know us, judge us and, thereby, control the possibilities of our becoming.

# Conclusion: How to Think and Act Differently

The arguments throughout this book lead to the conclusion that it is possible to develop a philosophically well-grounded account of the politics of truth that can provide a motivationally rich set of resources for activist engagement in practices of resistance. Let us briefly recap each of the main themes. The idea that we can discern the truth about ourselves and our place in the world, be it naturally or socially and politically, and use this as the basis to resist all those regimes of knowledge and power that try to keep us in our place through lies of one sort or another is a powerful, but ultimately unsustainable, account of the relationship between truth, politics and resistance. It is unsustainable because the account of truth upon which it rests, whatever the content of the truth claims, is blind to the forces that must already have forged the political scene within which one is trying to pit one's own truth against the lies of another. If we can not articulate the ways in which what we say, think, feel and do are always already governed through a series of rules and regularities that pre-exist our own awareness of the situation in which we find ourselves then we will inevitably be prone to replicating, and thereby reinforcing, the very systems and structures of power that we think we are fighting against so vehemently. This is the problem of dogmatism. That said, it is only one side of the problem. On the other side, if the truth will not set us free then there is the temptation to resign ourselves to a scepticism that will only end in defeatism. The tendency toward such scepticism is deeply entrenched in the idea that we can never locate the ultimate grounds of our claims about the world and our place in it and therefore we should simply give up trying to resist the systems and structures that determine our sense of who we are, no matter how much it pains us. However, simply accepting one's place in the world because there is no way of resisting it in the name of truth, is to cede the political terrain to the powerful. For those in power, those who benefit from the status quo or those utterly indifferent to their own condition this may well be enough. For those who feel the need to resist the ways in which we are defined and constrained by dominant regimes of knowledge and power, it is unacceptable. For this latter group, especially those within it that wish to avoid the pitfalls of dogmatism, the key question is whether or not interrogating the politics of truth, the idea that all truth claims have a political basis to them, will

necessarily lead to scepticism and therefore to defeatism. As argued throughout, this question generates the need for a critical account of the politics of
truth, one that will overcome dogmatic truth claims and sceptical defeatism.
Such a critical account requires that we are able to establish a well-grounded
critique of the politics of truth that can motivate practices of resistance. Developing this critical account has been the main aim of this book.

As the journey through some of the highways and byways of poststructuralist and post-foundational political theory has made clear, it is not a straightforward matter. On the poststructuralist side, we have seen throughout that
once we begin to excavate the assumptions that reside within our claims about
politics, truth and resistance there is a tendency for these assumptions either
to find a way back in to our critical conception or to keep digging away at them
until we risk losing sight of the practices of resistance that we are trying to
motivate and support. On the post-foundational side, we have seen that if one
wants to reclaim truth as a necessary feature of forms of politics that can challenge, even revolutionise, the liberal democratic parliamentary consensus then
one needs to rethink completely what we mean by truth. The inventiveness and
conceptual creativity of both positions is obvious: either a fully-fledged account
of immanent critique or a new way of thinking about how the subject relates
to truth must be established as rigorously as possible. Moreover, the source of
their respective originality is in the fact that both of these positions articulate
their novel conceptual schemes in terms of an event-oriented political philosophy. This is necessary in order to move beyond the truth about politics and to
embrace a non-defeatist politics of truth, as it is evident that we must make this
move if we are to slough off the last vestiges of all those traditional conceptions
of politics that identify the object of resistance and that, therefore, require a
notion of the constituent subject in order to judge it. Events must, in some
fundamental sense, have priority over and above the things we criticise and
our sense of ourselves as critics and practitioners of resistance to avoid placing
both aspects out of reach of critique. There are, initially, simple questions we
need to ask: what has happened such that we have the truths we have, today?
What has happened to make me think that this is the truth about who I am?
What may happen to change what counts as true? These are the questions that
unite the poststructuralist and post-foundationalist projects; and do so with far
reaching consequences in terms of how we conceive of ontology, epistemology
and practical philosophy, as well as the relationship between them.

But does this broadly shared territory mean that we have to give up on making a judgement between these two competing theories of the event? I have
argued that this is not the case; that we can and must come down on the side
of poststructuralism. The over-riding criterion is simple enough: a critical conception of the politics of truth that can animate practices of resistance must
avoid presuming anything that is beyond the reach of its own critique. The

first three chapters took the form of a journey towards establishing a consistent view of how this criterion can be met within the work of Foucault and Deleuze, one that ultimately ends with the figure of the learner as critic who can become the creative practitioner of resistance, the artist of the event. As argued at the end of Chapter 4, however, Badiou's version of an event based politics of truth can not meet this criterion because his procedural account of the militant's commitment to truth ended up resting upon a formal account of how one can be seized by the event that nonetheless requires a substantive account of such a procedure; that is, an account that is necessary to but effaced within his own philosophy. The militant must learn to be a militant even when seized by the truth of the political event. The person who learns how to critique and resist, on the other hand, has all the resources available to become militant as and when the situation demands; though such militancy, because secondary to learning, is without a dogmatic basis. It seems that basing one's politics of truth on (even a very novel concept of) truth will always lead to dogmatism. On the other hand, critique as a practice of learning is also the basis for learning as a practice of resistance. In the previous chapter, we saw how this can be brought to bear upon contemporary forms of algorithmically governed economic, social and political formations. The task, today, is to learn how the IF...THEN operations that govern so much of our contemporary lives function, and to conduct this process of learning by asking 'what if...we connect things differently'. In this sense, rhizomatics is the properly process oriented method that links critique and resistance, today.

Nonetheless, persistent questions remained regarding whether or not this speculative form of creative endeavour could provide the motivational richness that can engender practices of resistance to accompany an immanent conception of critique. Is it enough to say 'what if' when faced with sometimes overwhelming forces that will always seek to determine the shape of who we are, individually and collectively? Two features of the immanent critique of the politics of truth returned again and again when faced with this motivational problem: a) the idea that there is a poststructuralist account of the 'power of truth' and b) the idea that a commitment to learning is the basis of creative practices that do express resistance to the stultifying regimes of knowledge and power. The importance of the first sense of commitment is that immanent critique as a practice of learning does not simply legitimate an anything goes attitude in the name of creativity. Rather, it motivates practices of resistance in the name of creative attempts to find particular alternatives to the way things are, in the here and now. It is a commitment to resistance as the process through which one reveals the operations of the institutions of knowledge and power that oppress us by exposing the complex and overlapping events from which they emerged. Once these discursive structures are made visible one can then mobilise the power of truth to expose the structures that reconstitute the dynamics of those events in ways that sustain their oppressive functioning. However, this critical endeavour can only be fulfilled with and through a matching commitment to changing those dynamics from within by forms of creative experimentation that were labelled above as the art of the event. In making a difference with regard to how we think, feel, speak and act – in the here and now – we will come to learn how it is that all of these aspects of who we are have been and are determined by regimes with a history of their own emergence. If one is not motivated by learning how the power of truth can function creatively then one will always replay the old structures and forge new oppressions. In this dual operation, the creative practices of critique and resistance meet in a deep seated commitment to learning that will unravel dogmatic claims to truth and select among options for alternative ways of life.

But is this enough to provide an activist oriented perspective on how a non-defeatist politics of truth can be expressed? How do we think and act differently, today? It might seem that the activist must appear on the political scene ready formed; interests already determined or pre-established identity in need of recognition. But this does not match the reality of those who engage in practices of resistance, when considered from the perspective of what happens in such practices. Indeed, it is more likely that presuming the activist must be of this or that kind – individual, collective, intellectual, worker, or whatever – robs the activist of the potential to learn which, if any, of these identifiers fits the bill. It is much more promising, from an activist perspective, to engage in the process of becoming active and the becoming subject that this implies. That said, even in this sense we must be cautious, as there is still the temptation, as we saw in Badiou, to delimit what this subject position must become. The merit of the poststructuralist account defended above, is that the learner is both a substantive account of who the activist needs to be in order to sustain practices of resistance but equally the learner is not a fixed and pre-determined subject position because it all depends upon what one's situation is, what forms of knowledge and power are oppressive and what one must do, by which is meant create, in order to challenge them. As we saw in Chapter 3, Deleuze's approach to learning as a practice of critique means that we do not know in advance how anyone will learn. We do not know, therefore, what form their critique will take nor how this will manifest in practices of resistance. But we can say that they will form a critique and they will become a subject that resists. This is a properly activist oriented conception of how a well grounded, immanent, conception of critique can motivate practices that can challenge, and even revolutionise, the world in which we find ourselves; a world dominated by discourses that delimit our sense of who we are and what we can be. It is a properly activist oriented approach to what Foucault called a new form of critical philosophy: 'not a critical philosophy that seeks to determine the conditions and the limits of our possible knowledge of the object, but a critical philosophy that seeks the conditions and the indefinite possibilities of transforming the subject, of transforming ourselves' (1997: 152-3). This form of critical philosophy is not as difficult as we sometimes imagine and it is more practical than we might sometimes imagine. In the form of a slogan: learn the art of resistance!

# Bibliography

Adkins, Brent (2015): Deleuze and Guattari's A Thousand Plateaus: A Critical Introduction and Guide, Edinburgh: Edinburgh University Press.

Althusser, Louis (2008): On Ideology, London: Verso.

Badiou, Alain. (2000 [1997]): Deleuze: The Clamor of Being, Minneapolis: University of Minnesota Press.

Badiou, Alain (2004): Infinite Thought: Truth and the Return to Philosophy, London: Continuum.

Badiou, Alain (2005 [1988]): Being and Event, London: Continuum.

Badiou, Alain (2005 [1998]): Metapolitics, London: Verso.

Badiou, Alain (2008 [1992]): Conditions, London: Continuum.

Badiou, Alain (2009 [2006]): Logics of Worlds: Being and Event II, London: Continuum.

Badiou, Alain (2012a [2011]): The Rebirth of History: Times of Riots and Uprisings, London: Verso.

Badiou, Alain (2012b): The Adventure of French Philosophy, London: Verso.

Badiou, Alain/Žižek, Slavoj (2009 [2005]): Philosophy in the Present, Cambridge: Polity.

Balibar, Étienne (1997): 'Le Structuralisme: méthod ou subversion des sciences sociales?'. In : Tony Andréani/Menahem Rosen (eds.), Structure, système, champ et théorie du subjet, Paris : L'Harmattan.

Balibar, Étienne (2005): 'Le Structuralisme : une destitution du subjet ?'. In : Revue de métaphysique et de morale 25/1, pp. 5-22.

Beistegui, Miguel de (2010): Immanence: Deleuze and Philosophy, Edinburgh: Edinburgh University Press.

Boltanski, Luc/Chiapello, Ève (1999): The New Spirit of Capitalism, London : Verso.

Bueno, Claudio Celis (2017): The Attention Economy: Labour, Time and Power in Cognitive Capitalism, London: Rowman and Littlefield International.

Caygill, Howard (1995): A Kant Dictionary, Oxford: Blackwell.

Chomsky, Noam (1965): Aspects of the Theory of Syntax, Cambridge, Mass.: MIT Press.

Chomsky, Noam (1968): Language and Mind, New York: Harcourt, Brace & World.

Chomsky, Noam/Foucault, Michel (2006 [1974]): 'Human Nature: Justice vs Power. A Debate Between Noam Chomsky and Michel Foucault'. In: Rajchman, John (ed.), Chomsky vs Foucault: A Debate on Human Nature, New York: The New Press.

Chomsky, Noam (2008): The Essential Chomsky, edited by Anthony Arnove, London: The Bodley Head.

Clisby, Dale (2015): 'Deleuze's Secret Dualism? Competing Accounts of the Relationship between the Virtual and the Actual'. In: Parrhesia, 24, pp. 127-49.

Cutler, Anna (2013): 'The Museum of Now'. In: Dillet, Benoît/MacKenzie, Iain/Porter, Robert (2013): The Edinburgh Companion to Poststructuralism, Edinburgh: Edinburgh University Press, pp. 352-67.

Deleuze, Gilles (1986 [1962]): Nietzsche and Philosophy, London: Athlone Press.

Deleuze, G. (1988 [1986]) Foucault, Minneapolis: University of Minnesota Press.

Deleuze, Gilles (1990 [1969]): The Logic of Sense, New York: Columbia University Press.

Deleuze, Gilles (1991 [1953]): Empiricism and Subjectivity: An Essay on Hume's Theory of Human Nature, New York: Columbia University Press.

Deleuze, Gilles (1992a [1968]): Expressionism in Philosophy: Spinoza, New York: Zone Books.

Deleuze, Gilles/Foucault, Michel (1992b [1972]): 'Intellectuals and Power'. In: Bouchard, Donald (ed.) Language, Counter-Memory, Practice: Selected Essays and Interviews by Michel Foucault, New York: Cornell University Press, pp. 205-217.

Deleuze, Gilles (1994 [1968]): Difference and Repetition, New York: Columbia University.

Deleuze, Gilles (1995 [1990]): Negotiations 1972-1990, New York: Columbia University Press.

Deleuze, Gilles (2004 [2002]): Desert Islands and Other Texts 1953-1974, Los Angeles: Semiotext(e).

Deleuze, Gilles (2012): From A to Z (DVD), Los Angeles, Semiotext(e).

Deleuze, Gilles/Guattari, Felix (1977 [1972]): Anti-Oedipus: Capitalism and Schizophrenia, New York: Viking Press.

Deleuze, Gilles/Guattari, Felix (1986 [1975]): Kafka: Towards a Minor Literature, Minneapolis: University of Minnesota Press.

Deleuze, Gilles/Guattari, Felix (1987 [1980]): A Thousand Plateaus: Capitalism and Schizophrenia, Minneapolis: University of Minnesota Press.

Deleuze, Gilles/Guattari, Felix (1994 [1991]): What is Philosophy?, London: Verso.

Derrida, Jacques (1978 [1967]): 'Structure, Sign and Play in the Discourse of the Human Sciences'. In: Writing and Difference, London: Routledge, pp. 351-370.

Dillet, Benoît (2013): What is called thinking? When Deleuze walks along Heideggerian paths. In: Deleuze Studies, 8/1, pp. 250-74.

Dillet, Benoît/MacKenzie, Iain/Porter, Robert (2013): The Edinburgh Companion to Poststructuralism, Edinburgh: Edinburgh University Press.

Dosse, François (2010 [2007]): Gilles Deleuze and Felix Guattari: Intersecting Lives, New York: Columbia University Press.

Foucault, Michel (1965 [1961]): Madness and Civilization: A History of Insanity in the Age of Reason, London: Routledge.

Foucault, Michel (1973 [1963]): The Birth of the Clinic: An Archaeology of Medical Perception, London: Routledge.

Foucault, Michel (1977 [1975]): Discipline and Punish: The Birth of the Prison, Harmondsworth: Penguin Books.

Foucault, Michel (1978 [1976]): The History of Sexuality: An Introduction, London: Penguin Books.

Foucault, Michel (1980 [1977]): 'Truth and Power'. In: Gordon, Colin (ed.): Power/Knowledge: Selected Interviews and Other Writings, 1972-1980, London: Harvester Wheatsheaf.

Foucault, Michel (1992a [1971]): 'Nietzsche, Genealogy, History'. In: Bouchard, Donald (ed.) Language, Counter-Memory, Practice: Selected Essays and Interviews by Michel Foucault, New York: Cornell University Press, pp. 139-164.

Foucault, Michel/Deleuze, Gilles (1992b [1972]): 'Intellectuals and Power'. In: Bouchard, Donald (ed.) Language, Counter-Memory, Practice: Selected Essays and Interviews by Michel Foucault, New York: Cornell University Press, pp. 205-217.

Foucault, Michel (1997 [1980]): 'Subjectivity and Truth'. In: Lotringer, Sylvere (ed.): The Politics of Truth, Los Angeles: Semiotext(e).

Foucault, Michel (2002a [1966]): The Order of Things: An Archaeology of the Human Sciences, London: Routledge.

Foucault, Michel (2002b [1980]): 'Questions of Method'. In Faubion, James (ed.) Power: Essential Works of Foucault, 1954-1984, vol. 3, London: Penguin Books, pp. 223-38.

Foucault, Michel/Chomsky, Noam (2006 [1974]): 'Human Nature: Justice vs Power. A Debate Between Noam Chomsky and Michel Foucault'. In: Rajchman, John (ed.), Chomsky vs Foucault: A Debate on Human Nature, New York: The New Press.

Genosko, Gary (2008): 'Subjectivity and Art in Guattari's The Three Ecologies'. In: Herzogenrath, Bernd (ed.) Deleuze/Guattari and Ecology, Basingstoke: Palgrave Macmillan.

Groys, Boris (2016): 'The Truth of Art'. In: e-flux, 71, pp. 1-11.

Guattari, Felix (1995 [1992]): Chaosmosis: An Ethico-Aesthetic Paradigm, Sydney: Power Publications.

Habermas, Jurgen (1987): The Philosophical Discourse of Modernity, Cambridge: Polity.

Han, Beatrice (2002 [1998]): Foucault's Critical Project: Between the Transcendental and the Historical, Stanford: Stanford University Press.

Hardt, Michael (1993): Gilles Deleuze: An Apprenticeship in Philosophy, Minneapolis: University of Minnesota Press.

Hallward, Peter (2003): Badiou: A Subject to Truth, Minneapolis: University of Minnesota Press.

Hallward, Peter (2006): Out of this world: Deleuze and the philosophy of creation, London: Verso.

Harman, Graham (2011): The Quadruple Object, Washington: Zero Books.

Hawkes, Terence (1977): Structuralism and Semiotics, London: Routledge.

Hegel, G.W.F. (1977 [1807]): The Phenomenology of Spirit, Oxford: Oxford University Press.

Heidegger, Martin (1962 [1927]): Being and Time, Oxford: Blackwell.

Heidegger, Martin (2000 [1935/revised1953]): Introduction to Metaphysics, New Haven: Yale University Press.

Holland, Eugene (2013): Deleuze and Guattari's A Thousand Plateaus, London: Bloomsbury.

Hussein, Nesreen/MacKenzie, Iain (eds.): 'Creative Practices/Resistant Acts'. Special Edition of Contention: The Multidisciplinary Journal of Social Protest, 5/1.

Kant, Immanuel (1998 [1781]): The Critique of Pure Reason, Cambridge: Cambridge University Press.

Latour, Bruno (2004): 'Why has Critique Run out of Steam? From Matters of Fact to Matters of Concern'. In: Critical Inquiry, 30, pp. 225-48.

Lazzarato, Maurizio (2014): Signs and Machines: Capitalism and the Production of Subjectivity, Los Angeles: Semiotext(e).

Lévi-Strauss, Claude (1981): The Naked Man: Introduction to a Science of Mythology, London: Jonathan Cape.

Levinas, Emmanuel (1989 [1984]): 'Ethics as First Philosophy'. In: Seán Hand (ed.), The Levinas Reader, Oxford: Blackwell, pp. 75-87.

MacKenzie, Iain (2004): The Idea of Pure Critique, London: Continuum.

MacKenzie, Iain (2008): 'What is a political event?'. In: Theory and Event, 11/3, pp. 1-28.

MacKenzie, Iain (2014): 'The Meaning of Ideology'. In: Geoghegan, Vincent/ Wilford, Rick (eds.) Political Ideologies: An Introduction, 4th Edition, London: Routledge.

MacKenzie, Iain (2016): 'Ideology, Ideologies and Ideologues'. In: Bates, David/ MacKenzie, Iain/Sayers, Sean (eds.) Marxism, Religion and Ideology: Themes from David McLellan, London: Routledge, pp. 133-150.

Maniglier, Patrice (2005): 'Des us et des signes. Lévi-Strauss : philosophie pratique'. In : Reveue de métaphysique et de morale 45/1, pp. 89-108.

Maniglier, Patrice (2006): 'La vie énigmatique des signes : Saussure et la naissance du structuralisme', Paris : Léo Scheer.

Marchart, Oliver (2007): Post-Foundational Political Thought: Political Difference in Nancy, Lefort, Badiou and Laclau, Edinburgh: Edinburgh University Press.

Martin, Luther/Gutman, Huck/Hutton, Patrick (eds.) (1988): Technologies of the Self: A Seminar with Michel Foucault, London: Tavistock.

Marx, Karl (2000 [1845]): 'Theses on Feuerbach'. In: McLellan, David (ed.) Karl Marx: Selected Writings, Oxford: Oxford University press, pp. 171-4.

McNay, Lois (1992): Foucault and Feminism, Cambridge: Polity.

McNay, Lois (1994): Foucault: A Critical Introduction, Cambridge: Polity Press.

Moore, Jason E. (ed.) (2016): Anthropocene or Capitalocene: Nature, History and the Crisis of Capitalism, Oakland: PM Press.

Morar, Nicolae/Nail, Thomas/Smith, Daniel (eds.) (2016): Between Deleuze and Foucault, Edinburgh: Edinburgh University Press.

Nietzsche, Friedrich (1994 [1887]): On the Genealogy of Morality, Cambridge: Cambridge University Press.

Patton, Paul (2000): Deleuze and the Political, London: Routledge.

Polt, Richard (1999): Heidegger: An Introduction, London: UCL Press.

Rouvroy, Antoinette (2012): 'The End(s) of Critique: data-behaviourism vs. due-process'. In: M. Hildebrandt and E. De Vries (eds.), Privacy, Due Process and the Computational Turn. Philosophers of Law Meet Philosophers of Technology, London: Routledge, pp. 143-168.

Sen, Amartya (2009): The Idea of Justice, Cambridge, Mass.: Harvard University Press.

Smith, Daniel (2012): Essays on Deleuze, Edinburgh: Edinburgh University Press.

Sotiropoulos, George (2013): 'Here and Nowhere: Poststructuralism, Resistance and Utopia. In: Dillet, Benoît/MacKenzie, Iain/Porter, Robert (eds.) The Edinburgh Companion to Poststructuralism, Edinburgh: Edinburgh University Press, pp. 385-407.

Svirsky, Marcelo (2016): 'Resistance is a structure not an event'. In: Settler Colonial Studies DOI: 10.1080/2201473X.2016.1141462.

Taylor, Charles (1984): 'Foucault on Freedom and Truth'. In: Political Theory, 12/2, pp. 152-83.

Taylor, Charles (1985): Philosophical Papers, Volume 1, Human Agency and Language, Cambridge: Cambridge University Press.

Widder, Nathan (2004): 'Foucault and Power Revisited'. In: European Journal of Political Theory, 3/ 4, pp. 437-53.

Williams, James (2003): Gilles Deleuze's Difference and Repetition: A Critical Introduction and Guide, Edinburgh: Edinburgh University Press.

# Social Sciences and Cultural Studies

Carlo Bordoni
**Interregnum**
Beyond Liquid Modernity

2016, 136 p., pb.
19,99 € (DE), 978-3-8376-3515-7
E-Book
PDF: 17,99 € (DE), ISBN 978-3-8394-3515-1
EPUB: 17,99€ (DE), ISBN 978-3-7328-3515-7

Alexander Schellinger, Philipp Steinberg (eds.)
**The Future of the Eurozone**
How to Keep Europe Together:
A Progressive Perspective from Germany

October 2017, 202 p., pb.
29,99 € (DE), 978-3-8376-4081-6
E-Book
PDF: 26,99 € (DE), ISBN 978-3-8394-4081-0
EPUB: 26,99€ (DE), ISBN 978-3-7328-4081-6

European Alternatives, Daphne Büllesbach,
Marta Cillero, Lukas Stolz (eds.)
**Shifting Baselines of Europe**
New Perspectives beyond Neoliberalism and Nationalism

May 2017, 212 p., pb.
19,99 € (DE), 978-3-8376-3954-4
E-Book: available as free open access publication
ISBN 978-3-8394-3954-8

**All print, e-book and open access versions of the titles in our list
are available in our online shop  www.transcript-verlag.de/en!**

# Social Sciences and Cultural Studies

Ramón Reichert, Annika Richterich, Pablo Abend,
Mathias Fuchs, Karin Wenz (eds.)
**Digital Culture & Society (DCS)**
Vol. 1, Issue 1 – Digital Material/ism

2015, 242 p., pb.
29,99 € (DE), 978-3-8376-3153-1
E-Book: 29,99 € (DE), ISBN 978-3-8394-3153-5

Ilker Ataç, Gerda Heck, Sabine Hess, Zeynep Kasli,
Philipp Ratfisch, Cavidan Soykan, Bediz Yilmaz (eds.)
**movements. Journal for Critical Migration and
Border Regime Studies**
Vol. 3, Issue 2/2017: Turkey's Changing Migration Regime
and its Global and Regional Dynamics

November 2017, 230 p., pb.
24,99 € (DE), 978-3-8376-3719-9

Annika Richterich, Karin Wenz, Pablo Abend,
Mathias Fuchs, Ramón Reichert (eds.)
**Digital Culture & Society (DCS)**
Vol. 3, Issue 1/2017 – Making and Hacking

June 2017, 198 p., pb.
29,99 € (DE), 978-3-8376-3820-2
E-Book: 29,99 € (DE), ISBN 978-3-8394-3820-6

**All print, e-book and open access versions of the titles in our list
are available in our online shop  www.transcript-verlag.de/en!**